Praise for Jc

"A life of bliss is not only possible, bu
are all it takes to live the life of you
light that will help illuminate the pa.

—Sheila Kelley, actress, TEDx speaker, and author

"In *Joyful Living*, Amy reminds us of the inherent and critical truth that we can each embrace the transformative presence of Divine Love within ourselves."

—Tosha Silver, author of *Outrageous Openness* and *Change Me Prayers*

"I dare you to try and find 101 ways to talk yourself out of your rightfully deserved bliss. Amy has your excuses list covered, ensuring your day is nothing but an effortless marathon of self-love, good vibes, and joyful living."

—Emma Mildon, The Spiritual PA and best-selling author of
The Soul Searcher's Handbook

"Amy Leigh Mercree is on a passionate mission to support you in your quest to live life to the fullest! She's your cheerleader plus your guide to access the deepest truths within your soul. Her book is like a passport to joy."

—Kristi Ling, author of *Operation Happiness*

"Amy's mission is to help you infuse your life with bliss. We all want more of that! She takes you on a journey to create happiness on your terms. Grab her joyful book today."

—Chellie Campbell, author of *The Wealthy Spirit*

"Amy provides an inspired resource for self-love and happiness, and she shows readers that joyful living is truly possible."

—Dani DiPirro, author of *The Positively Present Guide to Life*

"Amy shares her path to living her joy and then gives you an easy road map to find yours. If you are searching for happiness and fulfillment, pick up this book and jump-start your journey today."

—Dr. Laurie Nadel, bestselling author of *Dr. Laurie Nadel's Sixth Sense*

"A wonderful resource for those looking to deepen their joy and peacefulness. Filled with suggestions and examples, I believe many people will find exactly what they need to enhance their inner (and outer!) lives through this book."

—Dina Proctor, author of *Madly Chasing Peace*

"*Joyful Living*…revs up our happiness engines and shows us how we can easily learn to live in a bright and beautiful state of Bliss-itude. I think it's wonderful that Amy is dedicated to encouraging readers to share their love and light with the world as she does. Keep up the wonderful work!"

—Eddie Conner, soul intuitive, radio host, and author

"In her well-written, light, engaging, and thoughtful book, Amy Leigh Mercree teaches us all how to live joy and cultivate beauty in our lives. I love this author and this book. Highly recommend."

—Patricia Leavy, PhD, best-selling author of
Low-Fat Love and *American Circumstance*

"Amy is an advocate for self-love and self-acceptance. Her fun book shows you how to find your own bliss and joy from a deep core of inner enthusiasm."

—Molly Ford Beck, founder of SmartPrettyAndAwkward.com,
cochair of the organizing committee for the 40 Women to Watch
Over 40 awards, writer for the syndicated Recommended
Reading print column, which appears in about 70 newspapers
across the US, and instructor at General Assembly

"Take an adventure of bliss with Amy Leigh Mercree. Her message sparkles with love and joy, and the good feelings are contagious. Her book will leave you with an elevated outlook on life. It's an atlas for happiness!"

—Sheri Fink, #1 best-selling author and creator of *My Bliss Book*

JOYfuL
Living

About the Author

Amy Leigh Mercree's motto is "Live joy. Be kind. Love unconditionally." She counsels women and men in the underrated art of self-love to create happier lives. She is a medical intuitive, author, media personality, and wellness coach who speaks internationally on kindness, joy, and compassion.

Mercree is the best-selling author of *The Spiritual Girl's Guide to Dating: Your Enlightened Path to Love, Sex, and Soul Mates* and coauthor of *A Little Bit of Chakras: An Introduction to Energy Healing.* She is also a writer and producer for film.

Check out AmyLeighMercree.com for articles, picture quotes, and medical intuitive information. Mercree is quickly becoming one of the most quoted women on the web. To see what all the buzz is about, follow @AmyLeighMercree on Twitter and Instagram.

Joyful Living

101 WAYS TO TRANSFORM YOUR SPIRIT & REVITALIZE YOUR LIFE

AMY LEIGH MERCREE

Llewellyn Publications
Woodbury, Minnesota

FIRST EDITION
First Printing, 2016

Book design by Donna Burch-Brown
Cover art by iStockphoto.com/57357878/©baramee2554;
            iStockphoto.com/25219161/©Peter Zelei
Cover design by Ellen Lawson

Llewellyn Publications is a registered trademark of Llewellyn Worldwide Ltd.

Library of Congress Cataloging-in-Publication Data
Names: Mercree, Amy Leigh, author.
Title: Joyful living : 101 ways to transform your spirit & revitalize your
  life / by Amy Leigh Mercree.
Description: First Edition. | Woodbury : Llewellyn Worldwide, Ltd, 2016.
Identifiers: LCCN 2016023384 (print) | LCCN 2016026871 (ebook) |
  ISBN 9780738746593 | ISBN 9780738750903
Subjects: LCSH: Spiritual life. | Joy—Religious aspects.
Classification: LCC BL624 .M455 2016 (print) | LCC BL624 (ebook) |
  DDC 204/.4—dc23
LC record available at https://lccn.loc.gov/2016023384

Llewellyn Publications
A Division of Llewellyn Worldwide Ltd.
2143 Wooddale Drive
Woodbury, MN 55125-2989
www.llewellyn.com

Printed in the United States of America

For my husband, family, and close friends, who laugh with me and make life sweeter every day.

Contents

INTRODUCTION

Bliss. What a delicious word. When you hear it, don't you just immediately crave it? Bliss is defined as perfect happiness. There are so many potential ingredients to perfect happiness, and they are not the same for each person. Finding your bliss is indeed a very individual process.

In *Joyful Living: 101 Ways to Transform Your Spirit and Revitalize Your Life*, I want to give you a full kitchen in which you can create a glorious meal of lifetime bliss. I'll provide ingredients and tools from all the major food groups: daily bliss, inner joy, heart opening, spiritual ecstasy, appreciating beauty, attitudes of gratitude, happy heart, creative inspiration, loving yourself, whispers from eternity, and feeling amazing. You can combine these ingredients in infinite ways to consciously choose to live a life of bliss and happiness. Ultimately, bliss is all about you—about how much you love yourself, how much you open your heart, and how much you consciously choose joy.

My Story

I was born different, and I always felt that way. When I was a young child, that was okay. I had an inner bliss and well of happiness and joy that came from authenticity. In grade school, I was diagnosed with learning disabilities. My handwriting was completely illegible, and I honestly could not physically help it. The way I perceived the world was different from most, perhaps because my mind was wired a little bit differently from others.

Being belittled, shamed, and made to feel like an outsider because of my learning disabilities was something I faced through many of my elementary years. My inner joy and happy heart were drastically dimmed. I didn't understand why I was so different, and I felt that somehow I was inherently bad. I felt ashamed to not be like most of the other kids.

Over time, I learned to cope. I found a teacher who valued differences, and that helped. In high school, I eventually fit in okay. But it took until college to really make a change. Freshman year, I flunked out. The same learning disabilities that had won me ridicule in grade school were stopping me from achieving my goals.

I had to make a change. I found a book about ADHD called *Driven to Distraction*, and it changed my life. I learned that I had to embrace my gifts and what made me different and harness them to succeed. I educated myself and conquered my challenges. I went back to college, made high honors, and had a successful teaching career for years, in which I related to the kids with love and kindness. I was able to heal the wounds from childhood. By being what I needed back then, a force of acceptance and love, I learned to love myself and celebrate my differences. I found my bliss and true happiness through self-acceptance, self-love, and finding the gifts in my own uniqueness.

During college I also apprenticed for years with a spiritual counselor. After college, I began my work teaching kindergarten on weekdays and working as a medical intuitive on weekends and in the evening.

I was ready for a new challenge and discovered that all of my unique gifts translated into a high aptitude for heart-based entrepreneurship. My differences paved the path for my success today. For me, everything comes from living from the heart, living joy, being kind, and choosing to love unconditionally as much as I am able. I am driven to share these truths with others; that is why I write books and speak to groups, to share that living from the heart with joy is a true source of happiness and unending bliss.

I know that life can be challenging. I know we all struggle. We all experience great highs and major lows. Many of us feel like outsiders or that we aren't good enough, successful enough, or attractive enough. Most of us have been through loss, trauma, pain, rejection, and fear. Ultimately, we keep going and striving to be happy and find fulfillment. *Joyful Living* is my love note to everyone who wants to live a life that feels good. And as the saying goes, "happiness is an inside job." I want to share what I learned in my life and from over fifteen years as a medical intuitive and wellness and relationship coach. Together we will uplift ourselves and the world from the inside out.

How to Use This Book

Joyful Living fosters an attitude that life is an adventure meant to be enjoyed. Too often in our high-pressure world we lose the soul in living. We rush to and fro, with little prompting to pause and notice the beauty in our lives. We might hear it is good to try to be spiritual or learn mindfulness, but the truth is that spirit is all around us and that connecting to it is the very essence of spirituality.

Joyful Living is for you! You're busy. You're complex. You're a good person, and you want to feel good. So, anytime you choose, you can grab this book, open to any page, read a few paragraphs, and do something to enhance your bliss. Now is the perfect time because you are wonderful and worthy of feeling blissful. And bliss is bountiful. It's all around you waiting for you to feel it.

This book gives actionable, practical tips to enliven our spirits and step into the blissful lives we desire. Bliss is pleasure and ecstasy mixed with contentment and peace. And blissful living is being radically happy, whatever is happening in your life. What is bliss? Bliss is actually one of the most spiritual and mindful states out there, composed of joy, appreciation, and gratitude for the wonder all around us.

Here you will find a book that you can open to any page and find inspiration. Each entry is short, easy to read, and can be used to uplift your spirit at any time of the day. No need to read in order, although you certainly can. It's meant to be enjoyed and savored on your own terms, whatever they might be.

Skip around! You might read an entry today, another tomorrow, and another a few days later. Consistently doing the exercises in this book will help you uplift your life on a regular basis. What gets attention gets done. And when you put even a few minutes of attention on your happiness, miraculous things start to happen.

Bibliomancy is the divination method of opening a book to a random page with the expectation that whatever is on that page is what you need to read at that exact moment. You can open this book to any page at any time and find a few uplifting minutes with a happy, healthy activity. Have fun and enjoy the process!

You might also choose to read the book in order or use the "Chapters by Category" section at the back of the book to find specific types of activities or topics of discussion that interest you. The possibilities are endless.

The intention of this book is to help you feel great as much as you can by revitalizing the heart, soul, and spirit. Choose bliss today and read on!

Mental Health Is Paramount

Your mental health is crucially important. The flip side of bliss can be depression. Clinical depression is a very real mental health challenge and should be treated by a qualified medical professional. There are times when these issues are far more challenging to alleviate than by just thinking positively. They can be chemically based or stem from major psychological challenges. This book is not meant to take the place of your medical or psychiatric care. It is simply a booster, a guide, and a support. You matter, and if you are dealing with major challenges like depression or anxiety, please find the help you need so you can feel good again.

Tools of the Joy Trade

Many of the activities in this book suggest you use a journal to record things. You might like to have a special joy journal or choose to mix your activities into an existing journal. Either way is great, and journaling can be a beautifully therapeutic thing to do.

When I have you do things like repeating a word or action a certain number of times, it is because numbers hold vibration. In each exercise this number causes the vibration that is most effective for the activity. If what I suggest feels right to you, do it. If not, skip it and take only what resonates for you. You know what is best for you.

Throughout these pages we are affirming how amazing you are and that you can feel happy in lots of fun ways. In every chapter there are affirmations that I suggest you say aloud and really let sink in. When we say something, it is as if our body's cells hear us. They listen up. So saying "I am happy and healthy" programs our cells to that idea and vibration. An affirmation is simply an affirmative statement said consciously and with intention in order to program our beings and lives to raise in vibration. Affirmations are an important, nonphysical tool of the bliss trade.

Use this book to find your daily joy. Daily joy is all about exploring happiness for yourself and tapping into the endless, self-regulating, self-correcting life force within you. Your life force is a power station of pure bliss. Power up!

World Joy

We all want to spread positive light and love into our world. We all want to see a world uplifted and a place where we help and care for one another. We want to leave a better, more conscious world for our children. We can be a part of the change we wish for our planet by sharing and spreading positivity. Positive thoughts and actions raise the vibration of our consciousness. When we raise our vibration, the vibration of the planet automatically raises too. It is natural law in traditions and religions of myriad countries and cultures. Sharing and spreading love, light, and joy begets more love, light, and joy.

We have a powerful tool for sharing positivity at the swipe of a finger—the Internet. What if amid all the noise online we were all a voice of light and love? What would happen? How much would we raise our vibrations and the planet's vibration? Let's radically shift our lives and our beings by sharing the positive and being blissful together.

To make this an easy and fun thing to do together, I've created a little shareable bite of positivity at the end of every chapter. Each one is 140 characters of bliss, just for you. If you love it, you can share it and spread the light. You can tweet it, post it to Facebook, Instagram it, pin it on Pinterest, or share it on your Tumblr. Each bliss bite will end with the hashtag "#joyfulliving101." The hashtag is included because we want your posts to trend. We want them to be seen by tons of people so the positivity will spread. Imagine joy and love trending! That is the kind of positive world we want to live in. Join the party. Spread joy.

Lots of love and bliss bubbles,

Amy Leigh Mercree

Sharing our love is the highest form of bliss.
#joyfulliving101

1. JUMP INTO FUN

Affirmation: "I seek fun and embrace it! I am present to the many enjoyable experiences in my life. I have the courage to push the envelope of fun and infuse my life with happiness."

Part of feeling joyful is having fun. Never underestimate the power of a burst of enjoyment and laughter to ignite authentic feelings of happiness. Experiences of fun are cornerstones of blissful living. Make a commitment to jump into fun today, even if it's only for a few minutes. Really hold to a promise of having fun.

If you prize fun and make it a priority, you will elevate your mood. You'll feel better about life in general, and your outlook specifically will be a little bit more positive. Every day will be a pinch sweeter with the delightful sweet addition of fun.

Fun can actually improve your health. Good feelings happen when you experience something relaxing, contentment inspiring, or exciting. When you feel good, your body gets a nice burst of happiness chemicals. They keep your brain and being tuned up and turned up. Enthusiasm for life results.

According to Christopher Bergland in an online article for *Psychology Today*, these are some of the major happiness chemicals and their functions:

Dopamine: We can release more dopamine by setting goals and achieving them. It is known as the "reward molecule." So if you aim to go to dance class twice this week and notice that you achieved your goal, dopamine may result!

Serotonin: When we have higher serotonin levels, we are less sensitive to rejection. Because we feel less sensitive to rejection, we take more emotional risks and put ourselves out there more. As a result, we might get more positive reinforcement that builds our self-esteem. To increase serotonin, set up situations that have meaning for you in which you can put yourself out there more and feel a sense of meaningful accomplishment.

Endorphins: These molecules are released during vigorous physical exertion and sex. Acupuncture has also been shown to increase endorphin levels. So get moving, get busy, or get acupuncture to feel the effects of these analgesic chemicals.

Oxytocin: This molecule is released by cuddling! It encourages and rewards bonding, whether with a romantic partner, pet, friend, or family member. Bergland explains that forming meaningful, close relationships and engaging especially in snuggling and physical closeness are things that will flood you with oxytocin.

Because your mental state has such a huge bearing on how you view your life, experiences of fun help you appreciate what a great life you do have, no matter the bumps and challenges.

Exercise: Daily Fun

In order to optimize your brain's chemistry toward joy, you need to make time for things that release the chemicals listed above. If you commit to your enjoyment and pleasure, you will find yourself feeling better. Make time for at least five minutes of fun today and every day. Cheers to your happiness!

Here are some ideas to have fun that take five minutes or less: Put on your favorite song and have a two-minute dance party. Bonus points if you sing along, loudly! Grab some markers and a piece of paper and draw something that makes you happy, maybe a unicorn, a fairy, a classic car, or a gnome. Add some doodles, and the more whimsical the better. Go outside and find a spot to do five power jumps. That means jump as far as you can! Grab your phone and imitate one of your favorite characters from a comedy. Text the video to a friend who likes the movie too. Do a quick cannonball in the local pool and make sure you yell, "Cannonball!"

So head outside, crank some music, run around, get busy, and jump into fun. If you have to, fake it till you make it. Enthusiasm for life will draw more enjoyment to you and make your life sweeter and lighter. Make the effort to find fun today!

Having fun is good for your health!
#joyfulliving101

2. Living Joy

Affirmation: "*I am made of joy! I am joy!*
My vibration is constantly raising, and I feel good!"

Joy can literally heal. After fifteen years as a medical intuitive, I have worked with thousands of people on healing body, mind, heart, and soul. This experience has led me to believe that joy is the highest vibration in the known universe. Joy is powerful. If you source your life from it, you will raise your vibration, raise the vibration of all you encounter, and have a blast by just being you. Joy is the magical elixir that opens the door to blissful living. Joy can heal. It can teach. It can humble us with its profoundness and show us that the world is really a benevolent place. Choosing to live joy is the best choice you will ever make. Start now by healing your body with the power of joy. Feel it and notice the change within you afterwards.

Exercise: Joy Can Heal

I have used this exercise with my medical intuitive clients for the past eight years, and they have experienced major results. Best-selling author Dr. Laurie Nadel even wrote an article for a magazine about how she felt that using this process helped her dissolve growths in her reproductive tract.

This exercise will teach you how to have a joy party in order to heal your body using the power of joy. The reason we call this a "joy party" is that we need a really high, super positive vibration to move the energy in your body. Imagine how quickly joy vibrates. It's electric! It can shake loose density in your energy body and in your mind. When you do something a little out of the box, like this activity, with a powerful intention to heal and raise your vibration, miracles can happen. Sometimes the most major healing isn't about tears and hard work; it can be about allowing, releasing, and relaxing into the benevolent, self-regulating, self-correcting power of joy.

Choose a part of your physical body you feel could use some healing. If you are feeling perfectly healthy, awesome! Then choose a part of your body you would like to give an extra blissful boost of joy. Visualize a ball of golden light before you. Say the word "yes" aloud to this ball three times, and tell the ball it is "joy" three times—literally say to this ball, "You are joy." Ask this ball to expand and encompass the entire room you are in and then the entire building and the area outside. You can do this wherever you are, even in the local juice bar. Place your attention on the area that you have selected for healing. Call forth ultimate power by saying aloud, "I call forth all of the magnetic resonance particles in the universe that love joy! Woohoo! I am about to throw the best joy party you have ever seen. Please help me. Join the party in my (area selected). Everyone meet there in five, four, three, two, one second!" Clap your hands together vigorously three times. (This creates a paradigm shift, which is a change at the most fundamental level in your body.) Visualize and feel the entirety of the joy ball condense into the selected area with a *whoosh*. Sing the most joyful songs, sounds, and tones. Maybe you are humming or singing a song you know, or perhaps you just want to make tonal sounds. Allow these to spontaneously bubble out of you. If that isn't quite happening, then fake it till you make it. Engaging your body with sound is another way you are shaking loose dense energy and making more space for the joy energy to fill you. When you add more joy energy, I believe you raise the vibration of your cells, tissue, and body.

When you have sung and toned your heart out (you are the entertainment for the joy party!) then wind it down a bit vocally, but keep the joyful feeling and let it become a peaceful joy. Feel the particles inside of you begin to sway in unison, as if they are holding hands by candlelight in peaceful communion, humming for peace, honoring joy. Lie down for at least ten minutes and feel yourself in the center of a multitiered circle of the humming, swaying particles. Drift off to sleep if you can.

You will feel when the party is complete. The joy and healing will remain for all time. Use this process as often as you would like, and allow the rest period after for the best results.

Joy is the highest vibration in the known universe.
#joyfulliving101

3. Love is everywhere

Affirmation: "*My heart pulses with love.
I am open to its healing and joyful effects.*"

All around, in every heart, love is there. It is glowing, radiating, pulsing in the heart of each person. The essence of love is present in every cell of your body. You are wired to love. From the chemicals in your body that reward you for feeling certain emotions, to the proven positive health affects of feeling close to another being, warmth makes life better. People often say love makes the world go round. And they are right. It keeps us moving and engaged in life. Love is the source of life. Love is universal life force. Love is flowing though your cells right now. Tap in and feel bliss.

Exercise: Love Inside Me

Close your eyes and place your hands on the center of your chest. Breathe deeply and relax for a few minutes. Try to allow your mind to calm itself organically. Bring your attention to your hands and where they contact your clothes or skin.

Simply notice what this area feels like. Does it feel warm or cold? Do any emotions come up? Does it feel tingly or pulsing?

Say the word "love" in your mind. Say it slowly. Savor it. Now, feel like the source of it is radiating from within your chest. Love. It is there, inside you. It's pulsing from your chest to your hands and back again in an endless circuit. Allow yourself to notice any movement of energy in that area. If you don't feel anything yet, that's okay. Sometimes it takes time to tune in to your body. Invite yourself to notice the love energy coursing through your body. It runs through every cell, every vessel, every vein. Feel it moving and pulsing through you. What does it feel like to you? What do you notice when you bring your attention to the word "love" while simultaneously focusing on your body? Do you feel the ocean of love energy woven through you? Let yourself feel it. Relax into love. Allow your consciousness to embrace and merge with the source of love, your own radiant heart.

Love sparkles within the shimmering jewel that is your heart.
#joyfulliving101

4. MEDITATE ON BLISS

Affirmation: "I am. I exist. I embrace my inner quiet and let it replenish me."

People are discovering that meditation is associated with improvement in a variety of psychological areas, including stress, anxiety, and depression. There's also research to suggest that meditation can reduce blood pressure and pain response. But how can you commit to it consistently? One way would be to do the activity below every week. It won't take long, and you will feel the blissful benefits.

Exercise: Meditate with Your Higher Self

Your higher self is the part of you that knows the state of joy without barrier. Here you will learn to connect with it, reaching that natural state. Your divine self is endless. It's your witnessing self. Meet it.

Practice stilling your body and quieting your mind. Pick your favorite spot and get comfortable. Try to get rid of as many distractions as possible by turning off the television, putting your phone on silent, and closing the windows if there's a lot of traffic outside. Some soft music in the background can be relaxing. Then, consciously connect with your higher self. To do this, simply state, "I connect with my higher self. Please teach me. I am open to healing and learning and blessing. I believe in your clarity and light."

Try visualizing that you are surrounded by warm, inviting light. Imagine that this light is your higher self, reaching out in order to strengthen your connection and to bring you closer to your natural state of joy.

Bring your attention to your brow center and repeat this mantra: "I am my higher self." A mantra is simply a word or phrase used for meditation in order to help concentrate on a desired goal. By repeating this phrase and focusing on your brow center, you are able to push aside the outside world and come closer to your inner self. When your attention wanders, just bring it back to your mantra. Sit with this for at least five minutes (if you like, you can set a timer).

Exercise: Simplify Your Inner World

Let go of the extraneous. Find your center. Enter into the mindset of simplicity. One thing at a time. Calm. Quiet time. Silent focus. No extraneous words, talking, or mind chatter. Just perfect, elegant simplicity.

What three things can you do right now to simplify and calm your existence? Write them down and do them. Open yourself to the inner bliss of a quiet, divinely connected mind.

Inner quiet can be cultivated.
Meditation is a healing balm to a
frazzled brain existing in a hectic world.
#joyfulliving101

5. find daily beauty

Affirmation: "*I am made of beauty. I notice beauty around me every day. I am beautifully blessed!*"

Appreciating beauty is all about seeing the bliss that can surround you if you simply open your eyes to it. You will learn how to glory in your world and enjoy diversity with happiness and love. Jump into beauty with both feet!

Every day there is a tremendous amount of uplifting beauty available to you. Your mission, should you choose to accept it, is to find it. It is all around. You reap the benefits of the beauty you sow, so create it. Appreciate it. Revel in the gloriousness of enchanting, evocative beauty all around you all the time.

You can appreciate beauty by simply noticing it. It can be visual, auditory, conceptual, olfactory, kinesthetic, or gustatory. One day it may be beautiful words of love from your spouse. The next, a flower petal as it falls to the ground. After that, a song or dance you witness. It could even be a sand castle built by a child or a haiku written by a friend.

You can create beauty by first pondering its meaning. Beauty is a combination of qualities that is aesthetically pleasing. Next, you can be an architect of beauty. Beauty brings bliss! Create a moment of beauty for yourself or to share, like a whipped cream heart on a waffle, essential oils to scent the laundry, kind words for a friend, or an artistic treat for yourself.

Finding beauty is about focusing on goodness. And goodness ushers in bliss. Engage your senses. Make a commitment to notice daily beauty. It's all around!

Exercise: Engage Your Senses to Find Beauty

Here are some ways to enliven your senses and experience beauty:

- Walk in a field of flowers or grass.
- Look at the passing colors as you drive down a country road.
- Light candles before bed and let yourself enter an unfocused state as you observe the play of light on the walls. (Be sure to extinguish them before falling asleep.)
- Walk barefoot in the grass or on the beach.
- Dance to your favorite songs with the windows open to let in the fresh air.
- Smell flowers on a walk in your neighborhood.
- Draw designs with colored pencils or pens.
- Listen to uplifting music.
- Notice the cold tingling in your mouth when you eat a popsicle.
- Feel the sun on your face as you walk to your car.

- Appreciate the texture of your clothing, like a soft sweater or linen pants, as you put it on.
- Calm your mind, observe the wind in the trees, and hear the pleasant sound it makes.
- Breathe in the steam during a shower and feel the warmth on your skin.
- Enjoy the fizzy effervescence in your sparkling water.

Open your senses and look for beauty. If you look, you will find it! Take ownership of your enjoyment of life and make a commitment to experience beauty and life's pleasure on a daily basis—your life will become ever more blissful.

Look for daily beauty. Let the splendor of life fill your senses.
#joyfulliving101

6. WHO CAN I THANK?

*Affirmation: "I am grateful for all the goodness in my life.
I thank life for bringing me so much joy."*

Attitudes of gratitude invite you to indulge in the pleasure of being truly grateful. You are blessed. You have so much to be thankful for, and appreciating it all draws more goodness to you. Gratitude is powerful. It is a force of expansive change for the better. Give it a whirl.

Be reminded of who you are now by sinking deeply into the feeling of gratitude. You were born spirit in body. You have lived and loved and laughed. Many beings have helped you on your path. People have come and gone, enhanced the quality of your life and taught you lessons. Who can you thank today?

Think of one person who has made a major difference in your life. How could you thank them? A handwritten card is so rare now that it seems extra special to receive one. Perhaps you could send one. Or you could do something else that is fitting for that person.

But what if you realize you want to thank someone you are unable to contact? They might be deceased or you might just not have their contact information anymore. Instead, you can do a gratitude ceremony for them to offer that energy to life.

Exercise: Hold a Gratitude Ceremony

Create sacred space. Do this by focusing on love and making a beautiful environment that is quiet and calm. Do some deep breathing to relax the mind. Now bring to mind the person you want to thank. Think of them fondly. Picture them before you. Express your thanks aloud in as little or as much detail as you choose.

Now say, "I release this gratitude to life to be correctly delivered in accordance with universal natural law, helping all and harming none." Feel the gratitude go out. When that is complete, say aloud, "I now disconnect from _____ as needed for my highest good and the highest good of all life. Go in beauty."

It is very simple to express gratitude. It is simply an exchange of loving energy. You can be conscious of thanking those you care for every day. Putting more gratitude out into life brings more goodness and bliss back into your life. Live gratefully!

Gratitude opens your heart to receive more goodness.
Then you give thanks and are blessed again.
It's an endless circle.
#joyfulliving101

7. WEATHER ANY WEATHER

*Affirmation: "I am worth the effort of creating a blissful life.
I choose to care for myself like a treasured lover. I love myself."*

The heart is one of the top things that create joy. Your heart feels bliss. Your body dances in joy. Your spirit soars with bliss. When your heart feels happy, that emotional, energetic organ experiences pleasure. Pleasure and joy beget bliss. And a happy heart is an essential ingredient to enhancing your bliss. Get a happy heart today!

Having a blissful life and a happy heart means having the life skills to weather any weather. Some of life's moments can be tough, some bursting with intense happiness, and some everything in between. Life engages the full spectrum of our emotions. Learning to weather storms and maximize sunny days is something that happens as we get better and better at living our peak lives. We can acquire the skills to surf all kinds of life's waves with ease and joy.

It is good to know what your emotional baseline is—that is, know the set level of happiness and satisfaction you feel. By figuring that out, you can discover how you are emotionally predisposed. From there you can raise your emotional happiness quotient as needed to find balance amid all of life's situations.

Exercise: Find Your Emotional Happiness Quotient

Answer the following questions.

1. Most of the time if I went inside and felt my internal environment, it would feel _____.

    A. Serene

    B. Excited

    C. Reserved

    D. Productive

    E. Joyful

    F. Restful

    G. Balanced

    H. Optimistic

2. On a standard day, inside I would be the following types of colors: _____.

    A. Pastel and light

    B. Bright and shimmering

    C. Muted and soothing

    D. Earthy and grounded

3. I feel _____ most of the time.

    A. Morose

    B. Down in the dumps

    C. Neutral

    D. Joyous

    E. Ecstatic

4. Which statement describes you best?

    A. I would like my average emotional baseline to be higher.

    B. I am satisfied with my emotional baseline.

5. Which statement describes you best?

    A. I would like to improve the way I feel when reacting to an external circumstance.

    B. I am proud of the way I feel when reacting to external circumstances.

Answer Key

Question 1

A or H: You lean toward liking the energy of the color white, symbolizing the divine. You are a sensitive soul and need to keep your environment gentle to maintain a positive emotional environment.

B or E: You lean toward liking things lively and active. You enjoy social pursuits and are great with people. Positive social interactions keep your emotional baseline high. You might like to add meditation to your day to help you relax.

C or F: You lean toward chilling out. You need quiet and calm to stay balanced. Too much excitement can be disruptive for you, so make sure you build in plenty of downtime to balance your activities. Make sure to try new activities regularly to keep engaged in life.

D or G: You lean toward emotional balance. You are great at navigating life's curveballs. You enjoy the good moments. Make sure you stay balanced with plenty of yoga or exercise.

Question 2

A: Your propensity is toward the positive and gentle. Stick with that and choose the light each day to keep motivated. You thrive on positivity.

B: Your propensity is toward the dazzling and radiant. Tap your inner energy to drive yourself forward. You thrive on enthusiasm.

C: Your propensity is toward the subtle and methodical. You take your time and make steady progress. You thrive on routine.

D: Your propensity is toward the organic and intuitive. Follow your gut feelings and stay focused on the present reality, and you will make your mark. You thrive on fecundity.

Question 3
A or B: It is critical that you make raising your emotional baseline a top priority. Make a commitment today to caring for and nurturing yourself. Launch a full-scale life-improvement and self-appreciation policy. You are worth it!

C: How could you raise your emotional baseline? Perhaps add one joyful act per day, every day. Try it!

D or E: You are in good shape. Keep doing what you are doing!

Question 4
A: Awesome! You are well in line with a positive emotional baseline. Keep at it!

B: You can raise your emotional baseline and feel even more blissful in your life. Try treating yourself several times per week to up your enjoyment of life.

Question 5
A: Commit to daily joy to improve how you feel each day.

B: Wonderful. It's still a great idea to commit to even a few minutes of daily joy. Your life will become even sweeter.

Getting in touch with how you are feeling at this moment will help you make conscious choices to improve your mood and outlook as needed to live a joyful life. You have the power to enliven your life. You're worth the effort.

Emotions of every color create the rich work of art that is life.
#joyfulliving101

8. finding simple pleasure

Affirmation: "I accept the blissful gifts
of beautiful flowers and plants."

Life is full of simple pleasures waiting to be experienced. All around you there are beautiful moments and gorgeous visages. Appreciating the beauty around you ignites the spark of your creative inspiration.

Creativity is a key ingredient to a joyful life. You must exercise and indulge your creativity. You can nurture your creativity. You would be even more joyful if you made sure to herald your artistic spirit. You must discover the part of you that wants to create beauty or enjoyment in the world through the aesthetically pleasing.

For some people the aesthetically pleasing will be artistic or visual. For some it will be auditory or made of words. For others it will be creative solutions and amazing inventions. Creativity is absolutely amazing and can be ignited at any moment.

Other key ingredients to your bliss are treating yourself as well as caring for yourself. Bring yourself to magical places and give yourself magical experiences. Trying to live a life of peak, wondrous experiences, whether subtle or intense, will help to create your bliss like nothing else. Why not combine your creative inspiration and your self-care into one beautiful bliss expression you can appreciate?

Exercise: Bouquet of Bliss

In this activity it's your job to create a beautiful, creative display of flowers—for yourself! You're going to be expressing your creativity and indulging your senses with the colors, scents, and textures of the flowers and other elements you select for your bouquet.

If you're lucky enough to have a bountiful garden of flowers, then you can do this pretty easily. If not, then there are several ways to go about it. One is to take to nature and pick flowers! Go places where you know flowers are blooming and gently pluck or cut them with love and care. The second method is to go to a flower shop. But, if you can, choose one that's really large and has loose flowers that you can go through and pick out yourself; don't choose one where you have to tell them what you want and they arrange it. Buy the flowers, take them home, and arrange them yourself. A third method is to create a silk flower bouquet by selecting faux flowers from a craft store. This is good option if you have allergies. You could also make paper or fabric flowers. It's all about your creativity.

Once you decide where to get your flowers, you are ready to start! You are going to create an arrangement to express a creative idea. Think about what idea you would like to express. Here are some suggestions to get you started: seaside magic; health, wealth, and love; orchid fabulous; wildflower wellness; passionate, red rubies; rainbow blooms; tribute to autumn; and winter abundance. Select your theme and think about what kind of flowers would express that. Gather those flowers in whatever way you selected earlier.

Now, take them home and find a beautiful bowl, vase, mug, cup, or other creative vessel in which to arrange them. As you put the water in, say aloud, "I infuse this water with the essence of bliss." Put the flowers in and arrange them beautifully. As you arrange them, talk to them about your theme, how it makes you feel, and also about the essence of bliss. Feel the energy and spirit of the flowers, and let that fuel your creativity. Thank the flowers for ultimately giving their lives to embody beauty and bliss for you. Imagine that the flowers are your own personal floral muses.

Take your blissful bouquet and find a place of honor for it in your home. Choose one where you will really see and appreciate the bouquet. Does it have a beautiful aroma? Touch the petals gently. What kind of texture do they have? Take it in. Appreciate the creative inspiration that fueled you to give yourself this gift of self-love and beauty, and accept the bliss of the simple pleasures in life, like arranging some lovely flowers.

Open your creative heart like an unfurling flower petal
and share your exquisiteness.
#joyfulliving101

9. seLf-Love

Affirmation: "*I am awesome! I accept my amazing, awesome self exactly as I am in this moment. I love myself.*"

Loving yourself is the fast pass to bliss! Self-love is the magical elixir that creates a blissful soul. This next chapter is dedicated to your lifetime journey of true love with yourself. The relationship that you have with yourself will be the most important one of your life. Treasure it and tend it with great care.

You are awesome! It's the truth. You are incredible, perfect, just as you are. You are a treasure of true beauty. It's a fact, and I don't have to know you personally to know it is true. You are innately perfect. There was nothing wrong with you when you were born. Then you grew; you learned. You changed in some ways. Some mistakes were made. Some great choices were also made. You are a rich tapestry of human being-ness. You are beautiful, just as you are.

How can this be? How can you believe it? Believe it you must: it is your key to a blissful life, one where you accept yourself, your flaws, your quirks, your secrets, your fears, and your talents. Self-acceptance is powerful. It empowers you. And it leads to self-love, the single most impactful thing in your world.

When you love yourself, life aligns. It is an amazing truth. The more you strive to love and accept yourself, the happier your life will be. You are an amazing, sacred, beautiful treasure just as you are. And you matter. You must be the one to assert your importance in your life. It is important that you have fun. It is important that you are rejuvenated.

You are lovable. Believe this, no matter your history and no matter what you are told. Know that you are worthy of love and that the first and most important place to get that love is from within.

Exercise: Accept Your Awesomeness

In this exercise you're going to practice telling yourself that you're just right and worthy, just the way you are. You're going to start shedding the negative images and ideas that society tries to push on all of us and start learning to love yourself.

Repeat these words aloud or in your mind now: "I am exactly right, exactly as I am. I am worthy of love, exactly as I am."

Exactly as you are. Think about that on a deeper level. Weigh it against much of what the media tells you. It is challenging to feel this truth, that you are exactly right exactly as you are. Rate how hard it is for you to feel this way on a scale of zero to ten, with zero being not hard at all and ten being almost impossible.

Keep repeating the statement, and see if it gets easier to feel its truth within you.

Accepting yourself is essential to having healthy self-esteem. Think of it as something that is crucial to your wellness. It's just as important as brushing your teeth or eating healthful foods to fuel your body. Accept yourself today.

You are perfect. Treat yourself like the being
of beauty you truly are.
#joyfulliving101

10. CONNECTING TO CONSCIOUSNESS

Affirmation: "My consciousness is eternal,
and I feel eternal bliss."

You hear whispers from eternity all the time. They happen in the still, quiet moments when your intuition shines through. There is an extraordinary, nonphysical world of love and bliss available to you. Explore it now, with an open heart, and experience true bliss.

Everything has consciousness. Everything is alive, whether it's a plant or animal or stone or even a man-made object. Everything has vibration imbued within it. The matter and energy that make up our world vibrate. They're endlessly moving, vibrating, and existing.

You can tap into consciousness in an infinite number of ways. What you're really doing is opening your mind, heart, and soul to the endless, benevolent, interconnected reality that surrounds you.

You are actually immersed in trillions of dimensions right now. Everything is simultaneous, and so everything you've ever been and will be exists in this moment. In addition, everything and every dimension are interwoven with where you are in space and time. The entire universe is infinite and endless, and yet it is contained in one single point: your consciousness.

When you connect with the infinity of your consciousness, you feel the ultimate bliss. You understand the interconnection between all that exists, and you feel that you belong. You are a part, a very important part, in an endless universe of consciousness.

In this chapter you will connect to infinite consciousness through something very ordinary: a leaf.

Exercise: Conscious Leaf Rubbing

Do this activity to connect with the infinite consciousness of bliss, which is a true reality.

Go outside and find a leaf. Choose one that is already disconnected from the plant or tree from which it came.

Stay outside or return inside. Place the leaf under a piece of paper, and use colored pencils or crayons to color back and forth over the leaf. An imprint or stamp will appear on the piece of paper. That is your leaf rubbing.

Notice how even though the leaf is no longer there, it has made a mark on the paper. Its shape is still there. Think of consciousness like that. It is eternal. After the leaf has disintegrated, the paper with the imprint will remain.

Your heart and soul are in union with your consciousness. Your consciousness is eternal, and it is connected with infinity for all time. Let yourself feel the infinity that you truly are. It contains infinite bliss.

Consciousness is eternal, and it is part of you.
#joyfulliving101

11. UNWIND WItH tea aND tuB time

Affirmation: "*I relax into bliss. I am content and full of joy.*"

After the hustle and bustle of your day, carve out some time for just yourself. You are important and worthy of love, caring, and time to unwind. Give yourself these gifts of self-love, and make it a way of life to maintain balance and eliminate burnout.

In this activity the healing properties of water combine with the invigorating essence of lemon, the relaxing and purifying energy of lavender, the joyful vibe of mint, and the sweetness of honey or stevia, symbolizing the sweet nectar of life.

Exercise: Unwinding Tension Bath

Take some time just for you. Give yourself the opportunity to relax and unravel any built-up tension. Then you will have more mental and emotional space to soak in bliss.

You will need some dried or fresh herbs or essential oils, and it is best to use organic ingredients. Use your hands or scissors to break up the herbs into rough pieces. This should be a quick and easy process. Gather the following:

½ cup fresh or dried lavender or 4–8 drops of therapeutic-
grade lavender essential oil

1 cup fresh or dried mint

1 fresh lemon

Honey or stevia extract powder to taste

Spring water

Start by placing your lavender and mint in separate small bowls. Boil hot water in a teakettle. Next, scrape ¼ of the zest from your lemon into a big mug and then another ¼ into the bowl of lavender. Then, slice your lemon into wedges.

When your hot water is ready in the kettle, pour it into the mug to almost fill it. Next, squeeze a couple of your lemon wedges into the mug and add honey or stevia powder to taste. Add about ¼ of your mint to your mug. Place the rest in your bowl of lavender and lemon zest.

Take your lemon mint tea and your bowl of dry ingredients into the bathroom and draw a warm bath. Light some candles if you'd like. When the tub is full, pour your dry ingredients into the tub and add lavender or any other any essential oils you'd like. Hop in and bring your tea to sip. Inhale the aromas. Close your eyes, relax, and receive the blissful contentment of the lemon, mint, and lavender. As you sip your special brew, absorb the sweet ambrosial essence of caring for yourself. Bathing is a healing ritual. Soaking is an enlivening treat, just for you. Enjoy your tub teatime and say this affirmation aloud while you soak: "I allow myself to gently release all tension and to soak in pure bliss."

A warm soak can wash away life's worries
and soothe an active mind. Choose self-care.
#joyfulliving101

12. how to feel happy

Affirmation: "*I let my inner smile enliven my being and enhance my health.*"

Happiness bubbles up from within. But what do you do when you don't feel it? You know that you want to. You might even know it's within you. How do you uncover it? Sometimes you have to dig it out from underneath dusty baggage like memories, thoughts, emotions, hormonal fluctuations, life situations, world events, and circumstances beyond your control. Life keeps happening. It always will, and it won't stop. It will be the dynamic, poignant ride it has always been. But what can change is you—how you deal with life, how you choose to live, and how you choose to be. It comes down to your state of being, where we source happiness from.

The external world can inspire your happiness, and it is a great place to start. Happy experiences are the best way to source the feeling of happiness. Here are a few to try:

+ Call an upbeat friend.

+ Watch a positive, nonsnarky comedy.

+ Get outside and breathe deeply.

- Walk in nature.
- Snuggle with a pet or a friend's pet.
- Work out (endorphins!).
- Cook something delicious.
- Smell some flowers.

Ultimately, happiness is an inside job. Start with the experiences above to remind you of the feeling. Next, smile. You may have heard of the "inner smile." It is a term used in Buddhism meaning a Zen-like sense of contentment. Try the following exercise to help you find your inner smile.

Exercise: Inner Smile

Start by doing something to inspire a happy feeling. Remember the flavor of that feeling when you were experiencing it. In this moment really be deeply present to the feeling of happiness.

Next, lie down or sit very comfortably. Close your eyes. Feel your breath moving in and out of your body. Let each breath be long and gentle.

As you exhale, blow the air out by pursing your lips like you have a straw in your mouth. Get into a rhythm with long inhalations and even longer straw-breath exhalations.

When you get comfortable with that, bring up the feeling you felt, the happiness. Be present to it and conjure its flavor. Smile gently. Feel your inner smile.

State, "I want to find where happiness lives in my body." Let your attention flow there and feel the happiness. Now, inhale into the spot. When you exhale, feel the energy flowing through your body. It is ever flowing, bubbling from a source inside of you. Use your breath to propel it to circulate through your body. Visualize this in concert with your breath.

Now, picture it billowing out around you, filling the space around you and eventually the room. Keep doing this for as long as it feels good. When you are ready to wind it down, say, "I am forever infused with happiness from the source within me." Then, let your breathing relax and go back to normal. Take your time getting up and returning to your day. Notice how you feel throughout your body. Do you sense that inner smile?

I have a secret. My inner smile is shining.
#joyfulliving101

13. Golden Tickets to the Life You Desire

Affirmation: "I choose my reality. My vision and actions create my life. I am an amazing reality creator!"

Remember the Golden Ticket in the book and movie *Charlie and the Chocolate Factory?* Your life is really the product of an amazing golden ticket! Of course, we have all experienced hardships. But the odds are if you are reading this book about bettering your life, you can read, you have access to books, you have time to spend on pursuits that interest you, and you have a positive attitude or are trying to have one. You are already so rich!

You can print yourself an array of new golden tickets. You can create your reality, exactly as you choose it to be, with your consciously chosen words and actions. The concept of the golden ticket is a representation of luck that arises from being pure of heart. It's actually kind of mythological. But the thing about luck is that you make the majority of it yourself. You do it by raising your vibration, honing your vision, and taking action to literally make your own luck.

Exercise: Make Your Golden Tickets

When you create a vision and intention for your life, you can multiply its power by crafting a physical representation of it. Then if you add a dash of fun or joy, you can really amp it up. The result is that you will harness your own inner power to create the life of your dreams. In this exercise you will make your own golden ticket.

Gather these materials:

Construction paper (yellow or gold is ideal)
Scissors
Markers
Stickers or anything else you'd like to use for decoration
   (optional)

The three immaterial ingredients for golden tickets are raising your vibration, honing your vision, and taking action. You can make as many tickets as you want with the following method. Repeat as desired.

First, raise your vibration. Take a piece of construction paper and your scissors. As you cut out a rectangular, ticket-sized piece of paper, say aloud, "I am joy. I am light. My vibration is rising. Rising. Joy. Joy is rising. Joy is rising in me." Keep repeating these kinds of sentiments as you cut out your ticket. By doing so you vocalize your intention for joy, and the cells of your body hear you and react accordingly. Your outer life is a projection of your inner reality, so as you focus on what you want and infuse yourself with joy, you strengthen your ability to create results in the real world.

Next, hone your vision. Take a meditative moment to reflect on what this ticket will be about. Pick an area of your life and what you want for yourself. For example, if it is career-related, picture clearly what this would look like. Is the vision of you at your own cake shop? Is it you in a higher position at your company? Is it you working fewer hours and having more fun? Once you have a clear vision, write out the specifics of the vision on one side of your ticket.

Last, take action. Really be intent on your vision. What needs to happen for you to get there? What steps must be enacted? If you wanted your own cake shop, the steps might include formulating a menu, creating a budget and a business plan, exploring financing, looking for a location, laying out a timeline, and seeking helpers and business counsel. Make an exhaustive list and transcribe it onto the other side of your golden ticket. You can write this on a piece of scrap paper first so that you can put the actions in the best order.

Add any decorations that symbolize the feeling you want to feel with this intention. The aspiring cake shop owner may want to feel happy and prosperous. You could write those words in colors that you believe go with the feeling. You could add stickers that have smiley faces to symbolize happiness. You could print out a tiny picture of a gorgeous, colorful cake and glue that on the ticket. Include whatever speaks to you and will make you smile when you see it.

Post this where you will see it, maybe on your refrigerator or bathroom mirror. Review your vision daily, and begin at least one action step per week. Stay committed to creating your blissful life. You can do it!

As architect of your reality,
you have the power to create it as you choose.
#joyfulliving101

14. Let go of fear and flow into Love

Affirmation: "*I let go of fear and immerse myself in an endless wash of love.*"

Imagine a replenishing, refreshing rainstorm made of pure love. What would it feel like to dance in that rain? Would you joyfully splash in the puddles? Would it be warm or cool? Would it be a color or clear? Let your imagination play with the idea of love rain, of glorious, rejuvenating, blissful drops of love dripping down your body and enlivening your soul.

As you imagine this love rain, notice if your body lets go of any tension and stress. You may feel your muscles relax. Your brain might let go of strain. Love is meant to be a central motivating factor in our lives. And yet, it's also meant to be a challenge to work toward. The more you can release and wash away fear (the opposite of love), the more space you make for love to fill you. Allow love to wash through you and dissolve the fear. Let yourself relax into the love that is present in each moment, and put down your baggage so that you can embrace bliss. Do this by simply allowing it, no effort needed. Just read these words and open yourself.

You might fear getting hurt again in romance, so you lug around these heavy, bulky bags full of past hurt. You keep them close so you are sure not to make the same mistakes again. But all the while you are spending years weighed down needlessly by hurt and pain. The fear keeps you from accepting love in its totality and especially from really letting yourself feel it. How about putting down your own baggage? Let go of the fear and embrace the love all around.

Exercise: Healing Love Shower

In order to merge with the spirit of love and open your heart, we will use your actual shower to help you receive a cascade of warmth and compassion. This will help you let go more deeply and open your heart. Read this exercise first outside the shower and gather any essential oils you have in the house.

Get in your shower and put the water on so it's nice and warm. If you have essential oils in the house, use some. Rose would be best, but lavender and bergamot are also good choices. Drop some oil in the corners of the shower and watch as you are wrapped in a fragrant steam. Be careful when you step in, as the oils can make the surface quite slippery.

When you're ready, slide under the spray. Ask your body to relax, and open your heart as much as you can. Say, "This water is a wash of love to heal me, and I accept it. I let my fears wash away and am refilled with love, bliss, and joy."

Watch the fears be washed away. Envision them flowing down the drain and being gently released. Sadness may surface. Let that wash away too. It will swirl down the drain with ease. Breathe and let go of any emotion. The flowing water helps it flow out. Just feel what comes up and allow it to move out of you. Just feel it, notice it, and let it go.

When you feel like that is all complete, switch the water to as cold as you can stand. Say, "I live love! I am bliss!"

The cold plunge at the end clears and seals your energy field, or aura. Step out refreshed and full of love.

In every heart a waterfall of love is primed to shower the world.
#joyfulliving101

15. cultivate connections

Affirmation: "I am made of universal love. I embrace my interconnected self and let it bring me joy."

Your spirit is what gives you life! It's your slightly indefinable essence that is at once universal and uniquely yours. However spiritual you consider yourself to be, you *are* spiritual. We all have a spark of the universal, sacred, and divine in us.

To enhance your bliss you need to cultivate a connection with the divine within you. It is glorious and vibrant. It is part of who you are. It's the electromagnetic energy that is woven through you and the entire universe that surrounds you. Everything is connected by an amazing matrix of energy. This is why you sometimes know who is about to call before it happens. It's why you can sense what others are feeling. Connection is something to be confident in even though you can't see it with your physical eyes.

Your connection to universal life force is something you feel. Universal life force is often called chi, manna, or ching, as well as energy or universal love. It flows through us all and through everything. It is self-regulating and self-correcting, and that is our natural state. The more we cultivate confidence in our universal, divine essence, the more bliss we can feel and the healthier we will be.

Exercise: You Are Universal Love

When you connect with the reality that you are made of universal love (and we all are), then you begin to feel the interconnected truth of your world. Today's challenge is for you to embrace interconnection. When you are out and about today, take a few minutes to feel the interconnection of all life. You might do this while out in nature, when walking the dog, or during day-to-day activities.

Tune in to the connections all around you. Notice the sights and sounds. Can you hear animals or traffic? Do you smell food cooking or the earth after a rainstorm? Concentrate on what you're experiencing with each of your senses and identify as much as you can. Feel it and notice if it makes you happy, uneasy, apprehensive, elated, neutral, depressed, joyful, or peaceful.

Make some notes, keeping the following questions in mind: Where were you? How did interconnection feel? How did you feel?

Allow yourself to feel universal love and interconnection each day. Notice how you become more attuned to your heart when centered in your environment.

Heart connection brings meaning to life and spirit to body.
#joyfulliving101

16. cheerful vibrations

Affirmation: "*I vibrate with cheer and delight in my cells.*
I let beauty heal me!"

You know those moments when life feels shiny and new? When everything sparkles? That is when you are vibrating with beauty. Everything has a vibration, from the rock to the plant to the pan you cooked your breakfast in. Vibration is simply how quickly the subatomic particles around you are moving. Emotions have a vibration. Experiences have a vibration.

The vibration of bliss is very similar to the vibration of beauty. And like fine wines and cheeses, they complement and enhance one another. By feeling the vibrations of beauty and bliss, you can find peace, contentment, and happiness and enjoy your life.

Colors have moods to them, don't you think? Do you like certain colors more than others? It is the color's vibration to which you are responding. A vibrant yellow makes you feel awake, alive, and happy. A deep purple incites feelings of originality, an active mind, and strong points of view. A sky blue relaxes you and inspires tranquility. A good way to think of it is that the colors inspire feelings in you that are similar to their vibrations, and certain people gravitate to certain vibrations.

If you choose to strive for happiness, bliss, joy, and positivity, your vibration will follow, and you will feel more engaged with life, vitality, and health. There are myriad flavors of healthy vibration. For some, the experience of splashing with a lively group in a crystal sea is the ultimate in positive vibration. For others, the most pleasurable type of vibration is a solitary walk through a moon-washed field of violets. These are very different but equally positive.

The experience of noticing and appreciating beauty has a special and positive vibration. It's a bliss builder!

Exercise: Uplifting Vibrations

When I first arrived on Maui in 2003 and drove my rental car out of the airport, I was surrounded on almost all sides by the majestic, verdant West Maui Mountains. The emerald-color vegetation was so vibrant. I crested a hill and saw the ocean glinting in the sun. Of course, I was struck by the loveliness all around me. And every day I try to see all of the gorgeous blessings that surround me, whether in a niece's laugh or a crescent moon. There is always something available in my life to uplift the heart and spirit, and I bet there is in yours too.

Go somewhere pleasant nearby, such as a park, a beach, an art museum, your backyard, or whatever place you find uplifting. Take it in visually, hear the sounds, notice what you smell, and focus on what you physically experience and emotionally feel. Partake of that bounty. What strikes you about it? The wind on your face, the arrangement of shapes in a painting?

Open yourself to the experience of beauty. Notice it. Where in your body do you feel it? Does it pulse, tingle, or warm you there? If there was a feeling associated with it, what would it be? Where in your body do you feel the feeling? Completely open yourself to the joy of this beauty. Let it get huge. Let it overwhelm you with bliss and joy. Feel it. Embrace it. Experience the vibrations.

The places in your body where you feel the beauty are places that are especially attuned to the vibration. You can bring your attention there when you want to appreciate the beauty of the moment.

Experiencing beauty makes life more vibrant and worth living. Try it and open yourself to it completely. Let the vastness engulf you, and realize you are a part of a radiant, beautiful universe.

Delight and cheer in life, and let it uplift and inspire you.
Spread happiness.
#joyfulliving101

17. Life is a gift

Affirmation: "I am grateful to be alive."

You've heard the saying every day is a gift, right? Although sometimes it might not feel like it, it's true. To be alive is a rich, poignant, complex, and blissful offering from life. Imagine that Earth is actually a super popular private school for souls to come and have an amazing sensory experience. It'd be like a person getting to go to a luxury acrobatic school if they'd really wanted to experience the highest trapeze for years. As a soul, coming to Earth is a great privilege. Envision a line out the door waiting for a chance to come to this school. Imagine it has the all-time best extracurricular activities, like sensory experiences, emotions, caring, and the power of love. Life is a gift of bliss, and you can open yourself to feeling the bliss of living every day. You can make the most of your time here.

Finding gratitude for being alive gives your life more significance, more meaning. Your life does mean something. It has meaning to the many whose lives you touch and to the universe of light and energy. You matter.

By giving of yourself you can share more of your goodness. Your caring matters. You may never know how much. The stranger you helped may have turned a positive corner because of your involvement. The friend who you made time for might end up having a more positive day because you cared. You can make a difference for another person, animal, or plant.

You can also make a major difference for yourself by treating yourself like you are a gift. Because you are. You are a gift. You matter. You are lovable. Embrace yourself and your life and be grateful for who you are, where you are, and where you've been. It made you the amazing person you are today.

Exercise: Thanking Life

How can you express your gratitude for life? One way is to craft a letter to life. Thank life for your existence. Thank life for specific things. Challenge yourself to be only positive in this letter. Only use affirmative statements. Try "Thank you, life, for my dance experiences," instead of "Thanks, life, for not making me play football so I could dance instead." Keep it positive.

We magnetize ourselves to more of that for which we express gratitude. Gratefulness attracts abundance. Thankfulness draws blessings. So thank life with your heart open. Accept thanks in your life, and honor what a gift your life is, has been, and will be. Life is truly a gift!

You are a gift to life. Share your bounty.
#joyfulliving101

18. Happiness is a state of independence

Affirmation: "I am joyfully responsible for myself, my own happiness, and creating a joyful life."

A happy heart can make anything possible. It can empower you to own your life, own your space, and be in your power. The statement of power through the heart, as opposed to the will, allows a feeling of independence. It's the feeling that your emotional abundance comes from within. It's an empowering feeling. You are empowered to make yourself happy. You are empowered to create your own bliss. You are independent of an external world that may or may not fill your needs. Instead you fill your own needs.

Happiness can be a state of independence. Bliss is a sacred testament to your empowered self. You sparkle and glow with the radiance of your independence. That is the reality. By deciding to believe that and be joyful about it, you reap the rewards of a joyful life.

By being you and expressing your own style and natural self, you stand in your power. You feed your soul with the affirmation that you are simply glorious. Your options are endlessly abundant this way. If you can dream it, you can do it, because you're powerful. This power can be a source of euphoria and bliss because it's balanced power. It's kind, caring power. It's blissful power. It allows you to bloom beyond your perceived limits and to dream big dreams as an independent, glowing, vital being. You are unlimited!

Do you believe in miracles? Your happy heart and an independent, empowered nature create them every day. You can immerse yourself in the playful joy of being powerful. Do this by affirming your independence, and dazzle yourself and everyone you encounter with your happy, full heart. Play with independence. Radiate with confidence and empowerment. Affirm your essence and honor the myriad, unique, prismatic colors of your own soul. Your happiness empowers you to own your life with authority, presence, and balance.

Exercise: Independent Happiness

Answer these questions in a journal and really give them lots of thought. Go deep with these questions. Mine your thoughts to consciously choose the ones you'd like to keep and the ones you'd like to allow to dissolve.

1. When you feel something is pleasurable (it doesn't have to be sexual), do you feel powerful? Do you feel shy? Do you feel proud or unabashed?

2. Do you feel happy in your core right now?

3. Who does your happiness depend on?

4. Who in your life negatively affects your happiness quotient?

5. Between zero and one hundred percent, how responsible do you feel for your own happiness?

6. What types of happy moments connect you with your heart? When is your heart happy?

There are no right or wrong answers to these questions. They're just intended as contemplation prompts. They are ways for you to suss out your happiness style, and they give you an opportunity to look at ways that you can take ownership of your own happiness. Look for ways to source your happiness from within. The ups and downs of life may rock the boat, but if you are buoyed from within, then you will stay above water in the sunlight of bliss.

The hidden keys of true happiness are individual responsibility and an incessant quest for joy.
#joyfulliving101

19. ENJOYING YOUR CREATIVITY

Affirmation: "I prioritize my creative pleasure. I enjoy expressing my artistic side and receive the gifts of doing so."

Creative inspiration is an enlivening and necessary ingredient to feeling bliss. You must ignite your soul with color and light and music to appreciate the diverse joy of this sensory world in which we live. Embrace your creativity with this book and jump into the endless colors of your bliss. You are creative!

When we are creative, we feel more alive. We notice colors and sounds and the rich tapestry of sensory experiences surrounding us. All of this positive sensory input has the power to make us feel good. Feeling good is one of the most crucial ingredients in a blissful existence.

How do you express your creativity? Every day you solve problems and map out the course of your day by resourcefully responding to external circumstances. You are actually already very creative. But what about creativity for the heart and the spirit? When you create something to express the colors and feelings within, you affirm the life within you. Some people do this through art, dance, music, poetry, cooking, mixing new drinks, making perfume, writing, gymnastics, choreography, animation, and even coding innovative websites.

Do you feel like you have placed emphasis on enjoying your creativity? Not just for your job, but for your own personal pleasure? If not, it's time you start. You will find yourself feeling more present to life and centered in your heart. You see, creativity is an expression of the heart and soul and the divine within. Letting that out is how you amplify it. Creativity magnifies your spirit, and it feels good.

Exercise: Find Your Art

One way to really amplify your creative pleasure is to try lots of different kinds of art. Try to work new creative activities into your month, maybe even two or three times a week. This can amplify your fun and energy with blissful creativity. Here are some suggestions to try:

- Take a Zumba class.
- Make a collage out of old magazines showing your life's dreams.
- Spend the day learning to play flag football in the park.
- Get some children's modeling dough and make sculptures.
- Put on ambient music and free dance with deliberately fluid movement.
- Invite some friends to paint pottery at one of the many shops popping up.

- Take a painting workshop.
- Create a new recipe in the kitchen (you can use a cookbook to help).
- Pull out your colored pencils and draw.
- Get together with some karaoke enthusiasts and exercise your pipes.
- Look up a cool makeup tutorial on YouTube and try it out, whatever your gender.
- Make fancy, fruity sorbet in a bunch of flavors, like raspberry mint, cucumber lemon, and kiwi green tea.

Delight yourself with imagination and artistry
and be inspired by life's beauty.
#joyfulliving101

20. Loving Yourself

*Affirmation: "I love all of myself in all ways for all time.
I am made of pure love, and it permeates all of my selves."*

Take a moment and listen to the word "self." Self. Say it aloud. What does it evoke when you hear it? What do you immediately think of?

Notice the tone or feeling of what comes up. *You* are self. The tone or feeling evoked has a lot of meaning for you, and it is totally individual to you. Did you think of the word "selfish" when you heard the word "self"? If you did, then you may have an innate belief that thinking of yourself is bad or shameful, that it is selfish to put value on your self. This is effectively telling yourself you are worthless. If this describes you, ask yourself where you got that message. Where was that example set? Maybe you were belittled as a child. Maybe you had a parent who modeled that their needs were nonexistent and only seemed to live to help others, so you internalized that anything else was selfish.

Caring for yourself is not selfish. It's basic and a skill that you must master to be ready to love yourself and even to love another.

Let's intone some affirmations to help us with this. Say the following phrases aloud: "I choose to care for myself. I am worthy of attention and caring. I *am* myself."

Exercise: Inhabit Yourself and Love Yourself

Now it is time to really inhabit yourself. When we incarnate, we all inhabit ourselves to various degrees. To live an effective life and love with your whole being, you have to fully inhabit who you are. You have to own your emotional space and who you are. When you own your space, you won't be bothered by energetic predators or people looking at you. You will be fully inhabiting yourself and your life, and no one else can affect that. It is the ultimate personal strength, and it is a gift you can give yourself today.

To feel what it feels like to fully inhabit yourself, say the following phrases slowly aloud: "I own my space. I own my body. I own my house (or apartment). I own my car (or bike). I own my life. I own my space and fill it with joy. I own my life and fill it with joy. I *am* my joyful self. Joy. Joy. Joy."

Joy is the highest vibration in the universe, and you can use it to infuse your life with positive energy. Breathe now for a few moments and feel yourself. Really be in your body and being and experience that you are worthy and full of joy.

Now bring your attention to the word "love." Say the word aloud: "love." What do you feel as you say it? What does your mind bring up as you say and think about love? How does your body feel when you think of love? Take a beat and notice. Be with yourself as you think about love.

Ideally, when you say love, you feel love. Sometimes, though, there are some other, more dense feelings in that mixture. Let's take a few minutes and sift those out so you can feel pure love in all of its divine glory. Let's unwind your past hurts and programming about love so you can feel the truth of this feeling.

Picture the word "love" in your mind's eye. Look at it. What color is it? Is it cursive? Capitalized? What is the background behind it? Be with this and feel the flavor of love that is coming up for you.

Is it the most joyful, upbeat, highly vibrational version of love you could feel and see? If not, then bring in your intention and say aloud, "I choose to infuse *my* idea of love with the pure truth of clear, divine, joyful love. I let this energy flow through my being and steep my cells in the highest vibration of love. I integrate joyful love into my life and body effortlessly now. It is done."

Let those words sink in. Allow yourself to relax into the essence of universal love. Let the tides of love within you shift and effortlessly self-correct. Feel the currents of past hurts subside and flow out of you. Simply notice this happening while you relax and observe it. Sense the pulse of love energy in your heart center, in the center of your chest. Experience love resonating out from your heart, tingling, pulsing, flowing, glowing. This true love is completely infusing your entire body, being, and life now. Say "yes" aloud now to true love energy. Again: "yes." One more time: "yes." You just said yes to love.

Now envision the word "love" in your mind's eye again. Notice how much more vibrant it looks, and feel the essence of true, universal love flowing through you.

Bring your hands up to your heart and say, "I am made of true, divine love. I integrate love energy into myself. I love myself. Every part of me is made of pure love. I accept all of me now. I truly, deeply love myself in all ways. I am worthy of infinite love. I am loved. I am whole. I belong to the heart of the divine."

Breathe and feel your beautiful, love-filled self.

Loving yourself is the single most important thing
you can do to create the life of your dreams.
#joyfulliving101

21. GROUNDING INTO GAIA

Affirmation: "*I thank Gaia for her support with great love.
I accept and receive the earth's sustenance.*"

Gaia is another name for the earth. She is a loving, helpful, benevolent part of our everyday lives. We exist on the surface of her body. The more we are connected to the earth the better we feel.

The term "grounding" refers to how present someone is in their physical body and how connected they are to the earth below their feet. The more grounded and connected to the Earth you are, the better you will feel physically and emotionally. When feeling well grounded, your mind feels clearer and less cluttered, and you view your life as manageable and positive. When you are not feeling well grounded, it is harder to concentrate, and you might feel spacey and not present to the moment. You can imagine how much feeling grounded and present will enhance your life.

Grounding is enhanced by being outside and being in physical contact with the earth. Try gardening, walking on the beach with bare feet, hiking through the woods, raking leaves, shoveling snow, resting under a tree and taking a nap, or breathing in the cool morning air on the porch before starting the day. Get yourself outside and eat foods that are healthful, like plants that are raw or lightly cooked (nuts, brown rice, grains, etc.). Drink lots of water—all drinking water has been inside the earth at some point—and get plenty of exercise. Taking slow, deep, cleansing breaths also helps you feel more present and grounded.

Learn to monitor how grounded you are at any given moment. Provide ways for you to get recentered and connected to the earth.

Exercise: Grounding for Health

Use the following meditation process frequently to help you get in touch with the energetic roots that tether you to the planet, nourish you, and sustain you. Read this aloud to yourself, or record it and play it back if that will be easier for you. Sit or lie down for this exercise. You may do this indoors or outdoors in a safe, quiet space to relax and experience.

Place your attention on the bottoms of your feet.

Feel and imagine roots growing out of each foot and out of your tailbone; send them into the earth. They may combine into one large root or remain two or three separate roots. All of these variations are fine, and you do not have to know which one is happening right now.

Feel these roots growing deeper and deeper through soil and dirt, through the matrix of rock and stone beneath you, and through aquifers full of water. Continue growing your roots down through the mantle of the planet. Finally, grow them into the core of the earth; feel them sucked into the inner core of the planet.

Held. Stable. Strong. Rooted. Feel the energy and vibration of the earth flowing up your roots and into your feet, through your tailbone, and up through your body. Feel it pulsing within you.

Hear the inner heartbeat of the planet. Hear it beating like a gentle drum. It is the pulse of the earth from beneath you. Merge with this interdimensional sound. Experience deep communion with the earth. Feel her love for you expand into each cell in your body.

All is right with you and Mother Earth. She has infinite strength and shares this wellspring of stability and strength with you, one of her children, for the earth is mother to every living thing on the planet. Thank the earth for this huge gift.

Allow your awareness to come back into the room or area in which you are sitting or lying. Feel whatever your body is touching—the chair, the bed, the ground. Wiggle your toes and fingers.

With your awareness fully in the moment and eyes open, feel your roots pulsing below you. Maintain this awareness for as long as you are able. Walk around still feeling your roots. Place your attention on the bottoms of your feet. Experience what it feels like to be fully present and grounded in the moment, in the *now*.

> *My roots are firmly planted in the glory of nature.*
> *The soil beneath my feet heartens each step.*
> *#joyfulliving101*

22. Designs for Life

Affirmation: "I surround myself with bliss.
My home is a blissful oasis that nourishes me and brings me joy."

You can design a life of bliss. One way is to create an environment that evokes bliss in your home. In order to do so, it's your job to define what bliss means for you. Is it joy? Is it happiness? Is it peace? Is it contentment? Is it spiritual ecstasy? Heart connection? Pure fun?

Exercise: Create a Joyful Home

Reflect on what equals a joyful life for you. Think about all the things you've done in this book so far that have helped you to define bliss, and then list five things that evoke bliss for you. One might be a feeling of joy. It might be a place or a type of landscape. It could be the experience of connecting with your archangels. It can be absolutely anything you want.

Really feel and think about your list. Ponder each item on the list and imagine. Think about what joy really means for you. What five essential ingredients make a joyful life? Write those down—it's important information!

Read over the ingredients list and then start with the first one. If you had to pick any color to symbolize it, what would it be? Go down the list and do the same thing for the other four items. What color matches the feeling and experience you had written for each? For example, maybe you have an item on your list like snuggling with your family. When you think of the feeling of the experience, perhaps it might remind you of a soft, gentle rose color. See if any of your colors are the same for your five items or if they are close in hue.

Get swatches of these colors together. You can find lots of wonderful color swatch websites online or paint sections at hardware stores. Put your five colors next to one another to make a joyful palette. How do they look together? You can tweak the shades if you'd like, so that the palette looks harmonious to you.

Now look at your home. Do you already have these colors in your home? If you do not, work on how you can decorate your home with these joyful colors to symbolize the blissful ingredients of your life. Focus on creating bliss in your home and your life.

You can make a poster using the colors of your five joy ingredients. Write a word in each color that is evocative of your five ingredients. For example, if your first joy ingredient is rafting down a gentle river under the stars and you chose midnight blue to symbolize that, then you could use midnight blue and write down the words "star rafting."

Do this on a poster with the five-color palette and five bliss items. Make it lyrical, poetic. Create a beautiful wall hanging with these colors and evocative words. Decorate your home with things that create blissful feelings in you.

Decorate your life and home to represent the vivid hues of your radiant soul. Share your brilliance.
#joyfulliving101

23. reawaken your inner child

Affirmation: "I love and commit to nourishing my inner child."

Within you there is a blissful, joyful child full of vitality. This part of you is wired to thrive, lives for fun, and is always up for an adventure. This part is the divine spark within you, the part that laughs uncontrollably at something silly, and the part that dances with abandon when no one is watching. And it is a key to living a blissed-out life.

When I made a decision to be happy after a tough couple of years, I realized that I needed to reconnect to the part of me from early childhood that was unfettered and joyful. I set about finding ways to do that. Some were silly, like rolling down grassy hills with my toddler cousins, which turned out to be really fun. Others were more logical, like doing an intentional art project that a child would enjoy. I made the little cartoon characters out of a kit with pieces you shrink in the oven, except I shaped mine into new shapes. That was fun too. I was working as a kindergarten teacher and nanny, so I had lots of opportunities to observe happy children. I knew I needed to recapture that essence for myself.

Exercise: What Kind of Kid Are You?

1. Imagine you are a happy child, free to spend the afternoon playing in whatever way you choose. If you had to pick one activity, which would you choose?

   A. Reading a favorite book under a shady tree

   B. Riding bikes with neighborhood friends

   C. Painting a mural on your tree house wall

   D. Going to the mall with friends and oohing and aahing at the merchandise in a colorful candy store

2. Which one word best describes you?

   A. Dreamy

   B. Strong

   C. Creative

   D. Sociable

3. If you could go on one of these beach vacations, which would it be?

   A. A quiet beach villa where you meditate and stroll the beach daydreaming

   B. A beachfront Zumba and weight-training retreat

   C. A pottery- and jewelry-making workshop week in a serene, coastal spot

D. A trip with friends to the beach, complete with dancing, pool drinks, and lots of sunbathing

4. When you think of relaxation, you most think of

_____.

A. A clear, relaxed mind

B. The feeling you get after a good workout

C. Witnessing something beautiful

D. Happy chatter all around

Tally up your number of As, Bs Cs, and Ds. The letter that you chose the most times is your primary inner child type. Also take a look at your runner-up letter for most choices. That is your secondary inner child type. These two types combine to create your own personal inner child type. Read through the descriptions and think about how you can affirm and foster the true you.

Mostly As: The Dreamer

The dreamer is ethereal, sensitive, and imaginative and likes to traverse spectacular inner landscapes of fantasy and ideas. Quiet environments often appeal to the dreamer and are a necessary recharge on a regular basis.

Dreamers enjoy reading, journaling, meditation, quiet time, calm environments, tai chi, gentle yoga, and knitting.

Mostly Bs: The Athlete

The athlete is powerful, grounded, physical, and rational and is most comfortable running, jumping, playing, and exercising. Physical activities from dance to team sports appeal to the athlete and are a very important outlet for acting out the kinetic energy within.

Athletes like to jump, run, bounce on trampolines, and push themselves. They try triathlons; 5K runs; CrossFit; trapeze class; high-energy, cardio hip-hop classes; boxing; a vigorous rollerblade around town; and anything that pushes their physical limits.

Mostly Cs: The Creator

The creator seeks to find beauty and make things attractive and is often a gifted artist, writer, musician, or designer. Making things is the way that creators feel useful in the world. Beauty is a spiritual experience for creators and an integral part of their life.

Creators paint, spin pottery, make jewelry, craft delicious recipes, choreograph dances, and write books and poems. They love to express what is within whether through dance, song, art, words, cooking, or any other artistic and aesthetic pursuit.

Mostly Ds: The Mingler

The mingler is most happy in a group of like-minded friends and loves to go to places where people gather for merriment. Being surrounded by others and a feeling of belonging equal security to the mingler. It is crucial to minglers to go out and about and have a lively group of friends with which to hang out.

The mingler likes to go shopping with friends, play team sports, join active health clubs, get manicures in a big group, and have big birthday and holiday parties.

Make a list of activities your inner child would enjoy based on what you learned about yourself from the quiz. Commit to starting to do things to revitalize your inner child today!

Within us all is a radiant inner child bathed in joy.
#joyfulliving101

24. you are effervescent

Affirmation: "*I allow my inner joy wellspring to be unbounded and free, to power me up, and to keep me radiantly healthy!*"

You are a bubbling spring of pure joy. That is your true state of being. You can be forever full with the effervescence of your own true nature. Being joyful simply takes practice. "How can you practice a spontaneous feeling?" you might ask. You're about to find out.

Exercise: Find Your Internal Wellspring

Take a moment to close your eyes and quiet your mind. Breathe deeply and find a peaceful moment. It's a challenge in such a stimulating world, but you can do it.

Once you have gotten centered and calm, take a moment to ponder how joyful you feel right now. Where would you rate your joyfulness on a scale of one to ten? Now commit to going deeper into your own joy. It's in there. With your eyes closed, breathe in and state, "I direct my breath into the center of my inner joy wellspring now." Breathe. Feel where the air and energy seem to go. Notice where they are in your body.

Breathe into the area in your body rapidly twenty-two times by focusing it and visualizing the breath going directly there. Repeat the word "joy" in your mind with each breath.

Do you feel the joy you set free now circulating within you? Whether you feel it or not, it is happening. Allow yourself to relax into it. Now say, "I allow my inner joy to flow wherever it is needed to raise my vibration."

Notice where it goes. Feel it go there. You may experience this as a "knowing," like you instantly know it flowed to your heart. Or you may sense it kinesthetically because an area of your body, like the back of your neck, gets hotter. You may start to see in your mind's eye that it flowed into your abdomen. Maybe you will sense a sound not audible to all human ears, like rushing water as it swishes to your forehead. The more you simultaneously relax and pay attention, the more you will sense.

Your body is wise and can use joy to heal and power itself. And you can optimize your systems toward joy. Use this breathing exercise to power up your inner joy and feel the wellspring within you bubbling forth. It is happening continually; now you can take hold of it. In this exercise twenty-two breaths are the exact right number to activate your inner wellspring and really get it bubbling with healthy, vital energy. I arrived at this number through years of working with clients as a medical intuitive and noticing what works best.

If you are out and about in your life and you'd like a joy boost, breathe one or two breaths into the area you identified as your wellspring and say "joy" in your mind while you do it. Feel the joy in you freed. Unbounded. Unrestricted. Expanding! Release your joy today!

Extraordinary effervescence exists within you,
waiting to be tapped.
#joyfulliving101

25. Letting Go

Affirmation: *"I let go of all that does not serve me*
with gentleness and ease."

Life is full of hellos and goodbyes. Some are happy, some poignant, and some emotionally difficult. People are emotional creatures. It is one of the gifts of being human. We have an extraordinary ability to feel so deeply. We also get attached because of our amazing capacity to feel. Though the richness of life is enhanced by our feelings, sometimes we need to let go of the old to make room for newer, higher vibrational emotions.

Letting go is a natural and beautiful part of life. You can let go of something today that has started to weigh you down. Your heart and soul know exactly what it is! All you will need to do is tap in. I'll show you how.

Exercise: Letting Go and Opening Your Heart

In order to let go of stuck emotions and heavy energy, we will connect with your emotional body. It's made of energy. This exercise will help you open your energy body so it can release what no longer serves you.

Feel your emotional body. It begins in your heart, the center of your chest. Bring your attention there and let yourself tune in. When you put your attention on the center of your chest, you might feel a pulse, heat, tingling, or simply a feeling that precedes any words.

Your emotional body is interwoven with your physical body and gets thicker and more voluminous at the very edge of your physical skin. Your emotional body extends out from your physical body about one to two feet, depending on your environment and mood. It is part of your aura. Your aura also contains your mental and spiritual bodies.

Feel your emotional body around you. Sense it by relaxing and opening to sensations in your chest and then all around you. If you do not sense anything, that's okay. It takes practice. This exercise will work either way.

Feel your heart within your emotional body. Feel how it is alive.

It is like ripples of heat streaming up from hot pavement in the summer, except it is cool and comfortable. Envision the ripples around you. Imagine the ripples flowing back and forth, in and out of you in constant motion.

Notice the edge of the rippling area. It is the edge of your emotional body. See the tiny sparks of electricity that come off it like miniature lightning flashes. Your emotions are electricity!

Send your awareness into these flashes of electricity. How do they feel? Warm? Cool? Tingly? Prickly? Buzzing? Sense them. How do they taste? Do you like them? Do you feel comfortable there?

Merge with the corona (an electrical halo) of your emotional body; allow your consciousness to feel and sense it. You can allow yourself to effortlessly merge with it.

Feelings may come to the surface, and you may even notice parts of your physical body responding. Stay present. Stay with the feeling of your emotional body's corona. Keep being present to what you are experiencing and don't check out. It is possible that your mind might wander, but keep bringing your awareness back to your emotional halo. Focus on the tiny sparks that are your emotional body interacting with the rest of the universe. This is emotional presence.

Stay in this state as long as you are able. Then, while still in it, move on to the final steps below.

State aloud, "I now let go of all that does not serve me with ease and gentleness." Visualize your emotional body and heart. Discharge any electrical energy that you need to let go of. Repeat in your mind, "I let go of all that does not serve my highest good."

When the letting go completes, rest for a few minutes. Then make sure you really come back to your physical body. Rub your hands over your arms, legs, and feet. State, "I am present. I am here now."

You have made space in your emotional body to experience more love and joy.

> *Emotions buzz through our beings like busy bees,*
> *giving us the gift of living vividly.*
> *#joyfulliving101*

26. choose to celebrate your spirit

Affirmation: "I celebrate my spirit with joy and playful abandon."

Your spirit is made of pure energy. Pure energy can be any flavor. Your choices, thoughts, feelings, and actions choose the flavors of your spirit in the present moment. The higher your vibration the better you feel. You feel lighter, more joyful, and more blissful, and your body is healthier. The highest vibration in the known universe is joy. By choosing joy, you can choose to raise your vibration. A spirit infused with joy feels good, and you can choose to celebrate it.

Exercise: Infuse Your Spirit with Joy

In order to connect with your spirit and celebrate it, try this exercise. It might seem a little undignified, but when you engage your body and voice, you bring more joyful energy into your cells.

Stand up. Stretch up by raising your arms. Now, bow low and hang forward, bent at the waist. Stand back up. March your legs up and down and let the movement become a skip. Skip around your room. Begin to create a song and use the word "joy" in it a lot. Sing your joy song and skip around.

Say aloud, "All the particles of joy in the universe, join me now and infuse me! I say yes! Yes to joy!" Keep singing and skipping. Create a dance to express the way the joy feels. It is freestyle and spontaneous. Now, say aloud, "I am my higher self. I connect to my spirit." Let the joy totally infuse your spirit. In this moment you may feel carefree and childlike.

You may feel something called the inner smile This is a concept from Buddhist philosophy. It means feeling peace and smiling contentment due to meditation or another spiritual activity done with intention. (See chapter 12, "How to Feel Happy," for more about your inner smile).

Revel in your joy for as long as you'd like. Keep this energy flowing in your body. Be joy and celebrate joy. You can choose to celebrate joy in your spirit and thereby heal your body.

Exercise: How Will You Celebrate Your Joyful Spirit Today?

Choose to celebrate your spirit to maximize your bliss. How would you like to celebrate? With a dance, a song, a piece of art or music, a treat, a night out, a hot yoga class, a juice- and smoothie-making meet up? You should do whatever will make your heart sing with joy. Celebrate your spirit by loving and feeding it joy.

One way I love to celebrate my joyful spirit is by singing and dancing around the house—the sillier the better. Sometimes, I really crack up my husband and myself with my conscious choice to be joyful. The thing about acting out your joy is it begets more joy.

Another way I like to breed more joy is through laughter. For me, that means making silly jokes and talking in funny accents. One of my favorite accents belongs to the red-haired child named Texas Ranger in the movie *Talledega Nights*. I imitate him to make people in my family laugh. Just the other day I was in the car with my mother, and she was affirming doing something for herself. I applauded her and then imitated Texas Ranger's prepubescent, Southern drawl: "I do what I want!" She laughed a deep, genuine belly laugh, and I did too. I was choosing to consciously spread joy and celebrate the fun of life, and so can you.

Celebration and laughter are two of the richest gifts of life.
#joyfulliving101

27. Rev up the spectacular

Affirmation: "I seize the moment and create bliss, right now!"

The spectacular in your life is the peak experiences, those moments you always want to remember, and life-changing days. These are bucket-list-worthy experiences. They are the pinnacles that we can use to help us strive for the best, most blissful heights of joy. Spectacular moments of sheer beauty might include standing on a massive cliff over the vast Pacific Ocean, summiting a mountain and eating snow, watching a top ballet company from the front row, surveying the city from the top of the Empire State Building.

The spectacular revs up our beauty sensors. It activates our bliss meters. It increases our ability to let joy and gorgeousness overwhelm us. Rev up the spectacular in your life today! Keep striving for these peak moments. They make life rich and exciting. Be spectacular and search for the pinnacles.

Exercise: Spectacular Beauty—Past, Present, Future

You will need a piece of paper and a writing instrument for this activity. You will be focusing on spectacular moments from your life in order to more fully appreciate their beauty.

Make three horizontal columns on your paper and label them past, present, and future.

In the past column, write down past moments that were spectacular. They can be anything from the time you were hiking and had to go through the middle of a herd of elk, to the moment you played your guitar on a stage before thousands of people and the crowd jumped with you in excitement. Or it could be the first moment you met your child or started your very first job. Reflect on your life and the small and large moments of bliss and spectacular experiences.

In the present column, list what spectacular experiences you'd like to have in the present moment. If you could do something spectacular right now, what would you do? It might be going for a new personal record in your lap swimming or something more adventurous, like dropping everything and going cave diving if you could arrange it. And it can't be something you'd do tomorrow or even later today; it has to be right now. What spontaneous things come up?

Notice how the idea of such freedom and spontaneity feels to you. Is it resonant? Or would you rather plan something first so that you are mentally, emotionally, and physically prepared?

Lastly, move to the future column. Here list the spectacular experiences you'd like to plan for the future. These might be vacations, like a tropical adventure in Fiji, or accomplishments, like having a best-selling book or releasing a jazz album. There is no limit here. Think big!

Reflect on what excites you about your future list. Did you let yourself go really big? Did you believe in your limitlessness enough to list massively spectacular experiences? And did you also embrace the day-to-day joy you can create through fun experiences and appreciating them?

Go back, read everything over, and process what this brought up for you. What types of things were on your mind? What are some themes for you around blissful experiences?

Choose one of your future items and take a step toward making it happen.

Now look at your present items. Which one could you go do right now? Do it!

Take the wheel and create spectacular moments for yourself.
Rev up the extraordinary in your life!
#joyfulliving101

28. ROOTING YOURSELF IN LOVE

Affirmation: "*I am rooted in the unlimited love of the heart of the universe.*"

Picture the heart of the universe pulsing with gorgeous, colorful, prismatic love. It is radiating feelings of joy, bliss, happiness, peace, contentment, and ecstasy, ingredients that make up love.

This is the true reality. Everything else we experience is just a different level of density that contains this love but also other things that might seem to embody love to different degrees. Right now we live in a world of duality. First, we have the endlessness of spirit and love available to us. Second, we also live in what seems like a limited physical world. That is the dual aspect of the world, but the truth is we are all unlimited. And that is because our hearts are in union with the center of the universe: love.

The universe is never-ending, so how does it have a center? The center, the love, exists in every atom, in every subatomic particle. It resonates through everything.

Love is color, light, sound, smell, taste, energy, photons, neutrinos, rays, quarks, strings—everything! Love is part of our

DNA. It's part of every star and every galaxy and every blade of grass. Love is the essence of life.

What if you planted your soul's roots in the center of the universe for all time? What might happen in a universe of endless possibilities? How much bliss would shower you in each moment? Give it a try.

Exercise: Root Yourself in the Essence of Love

You come from love and one day you will return to love. Spend some time in that essence now, the only reality that truly exists.

The heart of the universe exists inside of you. Close your eyes and journey there now. With your eyes closed begin to repeat the word "love" over and over in your mind like a mantra. You can sing it or intone it as well. Keep repeating and feel the center of your back and the center of your chest begin to pulse and activate. Allow the center of your chest to radiate the word. Feel like love is radiating out from the center of your chest in all directions, including backward, as you are thinking the word.

Continue repeating the word. Bring your attention to your consciousness, which you should feel right now in your brow center pulsing with the word. Drop it down into the center of your chest. Bring your full attention there, with the word "love" pulsing through you. Feel it wave and flow.

What does it feel like? Does it have color or light associated with it? Sense or smell? As you keep letting love intone from the center of your chest and your consciousness, let your consciousness take a ride out on one of those love waves as it's radiated. Feel your consciousness instantaneously enter a larger representation of the heart of the universe.

You just dropped right into the source, the heart of love. Sit there in the center of the universe in lotus position, like you're meditating. You still will feel your love pulsing from the center of your chest, and yet you are sitting in the heart of the universe. You're experiencing love within and without.

All this time, keep repeating your mantra. Rest in this for as long as you like. Dig your roots into it. Really be in the essence of love. Let it relax you. Let it calm you. Let it open the doors to ultimate bliss for you.

When you're ready, you can bring your attention back to the room. Drink some water. Wiggle your fingers and toes. Move your hands and feet and feel yourself become present to the reality around you again.

But keep the essence of love with you forevermore.

Love is the opposite of fear. It is free and transcends all space and time. Love is infinite.
#joyfulliving101

29. Living in the Present

Affirmation: *"The sun heals me every day and opens my heart to ever-expanding bliss."*

Imagine sunlight warming your face. Imagine bliss bubbling forth from a happy heart. Imagine you feel joy every day. Is this a distant utopia? No! It's the euphoria of living in the present. By living in the present, you are refusing to allow past hurts or future worries to weigh you down. They are not forgotten, of course; your past has made you the amazing person you are today, the person with the strength to face tomorrow. Part of that strength is being able to appreciate the joy and beauty around you and allowing yourself the freedom to just be part of it. You have the power to find the bliss in your own heart every single day. Your heart is filled with fresh, vital life force and brimming with love and nourishment, and it is waiting for you to tap into it. Imagine your heart filled with fluffy, colorful flower petals woven through rays and sparkles of glistening light. This is the reality and truth of who you are. You are filled with thrilling, relaxing, bright, luxurious beauty. It is your true nature.

Living in the present makes it possible for you to appreciate each moment. When you are projecting ahead and thinking about the future or reapplying the past, you miss the present moment. Being mindful of the moment lets you receive its gifts.

Appreciate experiences like warm sunlight on your face, ocean waves lapping your toes, or snuggling with a treasured lover or pet. Let experiences of joy and beauty infiltrate your heart. Unlock the doors. Open the blinds. Let in the light. Your heart is the key to your happiness.

Opening your heart to true happiness and the experiences that bring forth that emotion is the most courageous thing you can do. It brings forth feelings of freedom and soaring bliss. You can have that today.

Exercise: The Healing Power of the Sun

Go outside and find a spot in the sunlight. If it's a cloudy day, you might consider waiting until the sun is more visible, but you can still do the activity, knowing that the sunlight is simply muted but still there. If it's winter, you can don your warmest clothes and go outside or find a sunny spot inside and do the activity there.

Lay out a blanket and lie down, looking up at the sky. Observe the sky and pay attention to the light, no matter how muted it may be.

Notice the clouds, or lack thereof, in the sky. Notice patterns and dappled light from any trees. Notice the radiance of the sun and how it illuminates everything around you.

Notice what the sunlight feels like on your face and any other exposed skin. Does it feel warm? How does your body feel and perceive it?

Focus your attention on the sunlight hitting the center of your chest. Even if it's covered by clothing, that is fine. Feel that sun: let it penetrate your clothes and your skin. Let the sunlight flow into the center of your chest.

Let the sunlight symbolize pure source light. Even if the sun is muted, the blaze of source is still strong. It symbolizes joy. Drink it in. Let your heart pulse in joy, starting there in the center of your chest and expanding throughout your body. Fill up your entire physical body with the sunlight-joy.

Now sunlight is pumping through every cell. See it continue to expand and radiate out from the center of your chest, your happy heart, and allow it to grow and expand and pulse and radiate all around you, filling up your aura. Your aura is an oval shape stretching out three or more feet from your physical body surrounding you. This is your personal space. Fill it with sunlight. Fill it with joy. Imagine an experience or person that brought you great joy and source that feeling. Fill your personal space with the emotion and energy of joy.

Keep pulling the sunlight in through the center of your chest and pumping it out until your aura is so full it begins to revolve to the right. Feel it move faster and faster. Feel it revving up. Repeat the word "joy" in your mind as this happens in order to keep spinning it faster and faster and faster.

Eventually, it will reach a critical mass in speed and there will be a burst of powerful, healing, and illuminating sunlight-joy. It'll explode from your aura and go out over everything. This healing burst will rewire your physical, emotional, mental, and spiritual bodies to accept more joy.

Take the time as often as possible to enjoy the gentle, powerful healing of sunlight.

Be present to this moment and open endless doors of awareness.
Now is where the joy is; be here now.
#joyfulliving101

30. JOURNAL YOUR JOY

Affirmation: "*I journal my joy, and my joy expands exponentially forevermore. So be it.*"

Keeping a journal is therapeutic and creative. You have this blank page before you, and you can fill it with anything—your day's experiences, drawings, musings, poems, wish lists, dreams, goals, a log of the plants or animals you have seen, story ideas, observations, meanderings of the mind or heart, or spirit writing. A journal is fun and liberating. It is yours alone. The pages beckon you to share. Even if you aren't in the mood to talk, your journal will listen to your pen.

You can magnify your bliss by writing about it. Keep a bliss journal and let your heart and spirit have a safe space to express anything. Idea seeds will be planted. In a world of typing on keyboards, magic is wrought by committing pen to paper. Or if you are a high-tech type, you could always keep your journal on your phone, tablet, or PC. Whatever you like is what you get with a journal because it is one hundred percent about you. Your thoughts. Your dreams. Your fears. Your goals. Enter the world of personal expression in your journal today.

Exercise: Joyful Journaling

The purpose of this activity is to get you to express yourself creatively. You are free to be yourself and to write about whatever comes to mind. As you get more comfortable sharing your experiences, thoughts, etc., with your journal, you may even become more comfortable sharing yourself with others.

If you don't already have a journal, get one. It can be a simple notebook, something special that appeals to you, or a device. Once you have your journal, you can start writing about whatever speaks to you. To get you started, here are some topics you could write on:

+ The best part of your day
+ What you want to improve about your reactions to events in your life
+ Favorite travel experiences
+ A list of goals for the month
+ A note to yourself ten years from now
+ Your own definition of bliss
+ The top three most joyful moments of your life
+ Your most secret aspiration
+ What your favorite color symbolizes to you
+ Free drawing, which can be doodles, sketches, outlines, or fully detailed drawings

- Freewriting—just let your pen be totally free and write anything that flows out
- Free association of positive words that you want in your existence

Sometimes your diary is the perfect listener.
#joyfulliving101

31. List your Lovableness

*Affirmation: "I am lovable in endless ways.
I look myself straight in the eye with love and acceptance."*

You are so lovable! You have endless qualities that are endearing and that you can appreciate. Knowing yourself and accepting yourself leads to truly loving yourself. That power permeates your entire life.

Make a list right now of at least thirty things that are innately lovable about you. You can't help these things; they are who you are. And you wouldn't want to change them, because your idiosyncrasies, flaws, and quirks are just as valuable and beautiful as your talents, positive qualities, and propensities. You are lovable.

Keep your list of thirty wonderful things about yourself nearby. Make a new list and add to the one you have often. Affirm your brilliance. Affirm your wonderfulness. Love yourself. List your lovableness every week.

Here are some words to inspire your list of lovable qualities about yourself. See which of these resonate with you: lyrical, airy, ethereal, caring, kind, animated, quick, emotional, practical, loyal, blunt, conscious, direct, responsible, strong, grounded, and assertive. Use those qualities as starting points and keep listing your own unique lovableness!

Exercise: Loving Your Reflection

Part of recognizing how lovable you are is being able to look at your own reflection without judgment and just accept yourself the way you are. This exercise is designed to help you do just that.

Physically look into a mirror and look into your own eyes. Gaze for a while and disengage your mind. Feel energy flowing from the eyes in the mirror into your own. Allow communion with yourself on the other side of the mirror. Keep gazing. Relax your mind and body further. Unfocus your eyes. Let the image before you change, and remain emotionally unattached to it. Just witness. Just watch. Be open to impressions, feelings, sights, sounds, aromas, or kinesthetic sensations. Just watch and listen; gently pay attention.

Practice this gazing often. The more you gaze the more you will know, but the less you will strive to understand. You will learn to just be a witness to your true nature.

Write about your gazing experiences in a journal. Make sure to date the entry so that if you do this exercise more than once, you can distinguish when each experience occurred.

There is something lovable about almost everyone you encounter. Uncover it, and you will experience true compassion.
#joyfulliving101

32. parental acknowledgment

Affirmation: "*I am empowered and thankful
for my parents' love and support.*"

Being grateful has a major impact on your quality of life. It lets you appreciate the goodness and forgive the strife. It lets you be free of your past burdens and soar in a life of your choosing. Owning your life and being grateful for the good is empowering. It implies that you aren't a victim and that you have great power in your life. And it's true. You have all the power in your life.

Gratitude, especially parental gratitude, is so empowering. So many of your traits were passed down from a parent, either by nature or nurture. Whether it's your nose, your height, your temper, your disposition, your talents, or your drive, a parent or guardian likely shared it. You were shaped by the people who made you and who raised you, and for that you can choose to be grateful. For all the love they shared, you can feel thankful. Let go of everything else. Just keep the good.

Exercise: Letters to Your Parents

Now it's time to write separate letters to each parent or guardian. Really take time and list out everything you are grateful for that came from them, be it the soccer practices, the moral support, organizing your kitchen, or loaning you money when you were down. Create these letters with love. Focus on the positive.

You can deliver the letter if the parent is alive and accessible. If the parent is deceased, then read it aloud and know their spirit will hear it. If you feel too shy to deliver it in person or aren't able to, consider sending it by snail mail. The impact of the paper in hand will be more evocative.

Share your gratitude and draw more and more goodness to you. Many people have complicated feelings about their childhood and parents, biological or otherwise. That is okay. These feelings may come up. You can breathe through them and acknowledge the reality that no parent or guardian is perfect. There is no complete, fail-safe instruction manual for a parent to deal with the dark night of their soul or old wounds that motivate poor behavior. Try to find compassion for yourself and your parents and also feel your feelings completely. When you can, come back to find the blessings. You may have inherited a fabulous singing voice from an estranged parent or a drive to succeed from a less-than-perfect role model. Finding the gifts, whether obvious or not, will help you process your life more completely. This will foster integration, which leads to forgiveness, understanding, and true bliss.

You were born of two flawed yet beautiful souls.
Happiness is your birthright, and love is your guide.
#joyfulliving101

33. start with a story

Affirmation: "I let myself play in an unbounded world of creation on the glorious written page whenever I desire."

The therapeutic effects of creating stories are known in many cultures. Throughout history, stories have inspired us. We keep coming back to them, from *The Odyssey* by Homer and *The Old Man and the Sea* by Ernest Hemingway, to Mark Twain's satire and Toni Morrison's novels.

Stories allow us to be transported. Simply reading a story we resonate with will ignite our imaginations. Yes, the literary masters do it for sure, but so do lesser-known novelists and authors every day. Maybe you could too. Many of us harbor a secret dream of writing a book. Why not try it?

In 2003, I was that person who dreamt of writing a book. It took years, and I started several other books that I never finished. I wasn't an English major or journalist. I was a teacher and medical intuitive with an active imagination. But the practice of writing was addictive. Creating can be infinitely joyful. I want you to feel that joy if it is something that you crave. As Napoleon Bonaparte said, "Imagination governs the world." So I let my imagination be my guide. You can too.

Exercise: Write a Short Story

Writing a short story can be amazingly cathartic. It can be totally out of left field and have nothing to do with you, yet it can open things in your mind and heart that heal you and can make greater space for joy to bloom in your heart. Plus, it's fun. Follow this map.

Start with three characters. Are they human? They don't have to be. Jot the following down in your journal: their species, names, genders, and top two personality quirks. Just let this flow organically. Write down whatever comes to you and don't overthink it.

Next, decide the one event that the story will center around. Here are some ideas: a wedding, a funeral, a holiday, a breakup, a war, a dine and dash, a chance meeting, a hot summer day, a blizzard, the writing of a hit song, the opening of a shopping mall, conserving a coral reef, first alien contact on Earth, a bar fight, finding a new dinosaur species—you get the idea. Be as out there or ordinary as you want, and make a quick choice. This is just for fun. No pressure.

Start picturing your characters in the situation. How would they feel? How are they each different? Write or type a few pages. Let it flow, and if it doesn't, just keep going. "Jim and Jane walked into the new shopping mall and looked around." You can just write without being self-conscious because nobody will see this.

When you are done, read it over. How can you make it more wacky, more emotional, more intense? Add some more to it if you'd like, or let it be. A story is a quick, creative jaunt to rev up your imagination and entice your mind. Now you can reenter your life with a sense of mental revitalization.

Imagination is the dynamic catalyst for every breakthrough.
#joyfulliving101

34. Drawer of Love

Affirmation: *"I live love. I am made of infinite love.*
I choose love in each moment."

Part of feeling blissful comes from feeling the emotion of love. Love feels amazing! Some say it is the divine flowing through us. Love inspires interconnection, happiness, and passion for life. Sometimes love relaxes us and helps us feel centered. Feeling love realigns us with what is truly important to us.

From the center of all love, there is a vibration so luminous, so clear, and so true; it is a vibration of pure knowing. Infinity. This is love. The more you can feel it, the better your life will be.

Self-love is very important, and so is feeling love for others and the world. How do you live this? What do you have that symbolizes it? A souvenir from a love-filled vacation? A love note to yourself or another? A handmade gift from a child?

Exercise: Collect Love with Intention

Gather up all kinds of love objects from your home. These are things like greeting cards you have saved, shells collected from a pleasant day at the beach, and special treats you have bought for yourself or been given. Choose items that make you feel like smiling when you see them. The intention of this exercise is to have a spot to find objects of love to affirm your self-love and the love in your life. Add in some love notes to yourself.

We are going to reappropriate the "junk drawer" idea and instead create a love drawer. If you can spare a top drawer in your bureau, that would be a great spot. But if not, a drawer that you are near often will do perfectly. Now fill it with your treasures.

As you place each thing in the drawer, think of anyone associated with it and repeat the mantra, "I joyfully give and receive love."

You can revisit this drawer throughout your days, and just a quick peek will ignite feelings of love within you. Love is the most powerful force of nature. It is free. It transcends time and space. It is infinite, and so are you. You are made of love.

Life is a collection of experiences.
Stockpile those wrought with love like the treasures they are.
#joyfulliving101

35. identify your gifts

Affirmation: "*I recognize my gifts and optimize them.
I accept my total being and honor all parts of myself.*"

You are gifted! Believe it. Everyone has unique and amazing gifts within waiting to be harnessed. The secret is to identify them. You may be an artistic amazement. You may be a musical marvel. You may be a caring comrade. You might be a hilarious human. You might be an innovative and interesting person. You might be smart and sassy or quiet and deep. There is an endless array of wonderful qualities, and we all have some of them.

We all have gifts and talents. We have propensities and ways we can enliven ourselves and give back to our communities. Let's identify some of yours!

Exercise: Find Your Gifts

The following quiz is meant to get you thinking about yourself and to breed self-awareness. There are three parts to it. Do all three parts to really get deep and know yourself and the ways that you can bring joy to your world.

Part One: Free Association

Look at each of these words and free associate: what comes to mind as a first impulse when you see each word? Write it down.

1. Effort
2. Dreaming
3. Sparkles
4. Life's purpose
5. Technology
6. Group activities
7. Vanilla
8. Spicy
9. Community
10. Earth

Part Two: True or False

1. I consider myself confident. T or F
2. I like to be subtle. T or F
3. My style is obvious. T or F
4. I like to be the center of attention. T or F
5. I like to dance at weddings. T or F
6. My gifts are well defined. T or F
7. I learn from my mistakes and get better. T or F
8. I try to stand out from the crowd. T or F

9. I like to hide in the background and observe people quietly. T or F

10. My life is calm and well ordered. T or F

Part Three: Your Special Gifts

1. What was your favorite subject in school?

2. What was your favorite childhood hobby?

3. What does your family know you as the go-to person for? (sewing, a heart-to-heart, laughter, etc.)

4. What are you passionate about?

5. How do you want to spend your time?

6. In a perfect world, if you could do absolutely anything tomorrow, what would it be?

7. What have you been professionally praised for?

8. What do you like about yourself?

9. What is your best feature?

10. What celebrity are you most like?

Answer Key

Part One

What themes or words came up for you? Look at how your brain worked.

Linear: Was it linear and obvious? Maybe you wrote "Vanilla—*chocolate*" or "Spicy—*food*."

Abstract: Was it abstract and unexpected? Like "Vanilla—*confetti*" or "Spicy—*brick red*."

Quirky: Was it quirky, and did it make you laugh? Like "Vanilla—*white bread lover*" or "Spicy—*bathroom break!*"

Or are you indefinable? How mysterious.

Part Two

Add up your points using the key to find your self-confidence level.

1. T=4, F=0
2. T=1, F=6
3. T=3, F=5
4. T=7, F=1
5. T=4, F=0
6. T=4, F=3
7. T=5, F=1
8. T=4, F=1
9. T=1, F=3
10. T=3, F=2

35–45: Self-Esteem Expert

You are a master at self-confidence. Keep up the good work and know how gifted you are!

24–34: Self-Assurance Apprentice

You are learning to be confident and recognize your gifts. Keep at it!

13–23: Self-Confidence Student

It's time for a self-esteem infusion, stat! Believe in yourself now. You are gifted. Let part three help you mine your bountiful unique gifts.

Part Three

Look at your answers and go within, be introspective about them. What patterns do you see? What is a common thread in a lot of your answers? Is it your style? Your artistic ability? Your heart-centered approach to life? Your skill at getting things done? Are you known for your way with words? Which of your answers are similar? Notice your best qualities, your achievements, and your ways of bringing joy to others. Make a list of what your answers have in common. If you love music, your nieces always want you to sing songs for them, you loved chorus in middle school, and the idea of singing every day lifts your heart, then you know singing is a major gift to explore. Maybe you could join the local choral society. Whatever your gifts are, appreciate yourself. You are a gift. Let yourself bring you joy!

When you consciously choose to do what you love,
life becomes a pleasure and ceases to be a chore.
#joyfulliving101

36. more and more every day

Affirmation: "I choose to love more and more every day."

Bring the action of love into your life by choosing your mindset and following it up with actions every day. Every day is a potential gift of love. You can choose to be in a mindset and heartset of love and light. Every time you choose love, you allow your heart to relax and open a bit more.

Each day you have the opportunity to open your heart to more love. If you choose to do this, you will drastically increase your quality of life. Your relationships will get smoother. Your life will become more joyful. You will feel more connected to your world. Opening your heart to love is the most health-promoting, philanthropic, courageous thing you will ever do. And it is a never-ending process. The rewards will astound you.

To open each day, you can choose love. Every morning you can rise with the attitude that you are ready for more love, that you are open to giving more and receiving more, and that you are ready to jump into life with both feet and dance to the rhythm of love.

The opposite of love is fear, and fear keeps us from opening our hearts to their natural state: wide open. Fear can invade us if we let it, but there is good news. All it takes to dissipate fear is one spark of love. The light of one candle can dissolve infinite darkness. The light inside you can vaporize all the fear. Just focus on the love. Feel the love. Choose love. Live love. Be love. Let your heart be open and fearless as you let yourself go into the endless, benevolent abyss of pure, divine love. It is simultaneously within you and surrounding you infinitely. You are infinite. You are love.

Exercise: Emotional Safety

In order to be open to more and more love, you need to feel emotionally safe. If you can get to that place, you will live a fuller, richer, happier life.

Create an internal environment of emotional safety for yourself by enacting the following steps:

Decree and decide that you are sacred by saying aloud three times, "I am sacred." "Sacred" means special, precious, and a treasure of true beauty. It also means worthy of respect and care. By saying the words aloud, your cells hear them and respond. Saying something three times strengthens and magnifies its power.

Act through a perspective of honoring your sacredness. Make each choice through that perspective. Ask yourself, "I am sacred and honor and respect myself. Will this choice only help me and not harm me in any way?"

Notice your self-talk. Speak to yourself (aloud and in your inner narrative) only with kindness.

Next, understand and internalize that all others are sacred —people, animals, and plants. Every living thing is a radiant expression of love.

Act and speak through the perspective of seeing all others as sacred. That means do not talk behind people's backs and treat everyone you encounter with respect and care.

Only choose to spend time with people who see you as sacred or worthy of respect and caring. Ask yourself if someone you are going to spend time with treats you well. Do you feel good in their presence? Do you feel mutual respect with this person? Choose your relationships with love and care for yourself.

Let yourself begin to trust your judgment because you see yourself as sacred and act from that point of view. When you are confident that you will make choices that respect and honor who you are, you can relax into emotional safety and learn to trust your judgment.

Emotional safety is feeling internally secure
and confident in your life.
#joyfulliving101

37. meeting your spirit

Affirmation: "My spirit is joyful, and I love my higher self. I am my higher self."

Your spirit has a unique essence. It is your divine spark. Your special soul-flame of existence. No soul is the same, yet we are all the same.

You can learn to feel your distinctive spirit. It may be sparkling or subtle, jewellike or watery, crystalline or fresh, happy or serene. You probably meet your spirit self in your dreams. Most people's spirits make contact in the quiet moments and the dreamtime. You can maximize those close encounters with your spirit and learn to have them consciously while awake. There is lots of value in all the ways you meet your spirit. Meeting your spirit allows you to get to know the real, blissful you because joy is your natural state. You may have lost touch with it, but getting back to it will feel like the most natural thing in the world once you are there.

Exercise: Journey into Your Spirit

In this exercise you will directly meet your spirit in order to reconnect with the spiritual essence of your being. This will help you feel connected to yourself in a deeper way, which builds your self-esteem and increases feelings of satisfaction with life.

It's time to meet your spirit. Lie down comfortably in a quiet space. Cover your eyes with a light cloth to block out the play of light on your eyelids. Use your hands to lightly drum on your thighs. Ideally, it will sound like rhythmic horse hooves at a moderate gallop. Do this consistently, and do not vary the tempo too much once you get it.

Drum on your body for a few minutes and really go into the drumming. Let your consciousness melt into the sound, and, at the same time, put your hands and arms on autopilot so they keep drumming with minimal attention from you. Drumming sounds change your brainwaves and bring them into a state in which you can spirit travel.

Envision yourself standing up, and see a lustrous golden cord hanging down before you. Before you climb up, say aloud, "I ask that this journey experience be for the highest good of all life and in accordance with universal natural law, helping all and harming none, and that I be fully protected during this process."

Keep drumming and climb up the golden cord easily. Repeat in your mind, "Journey to my spirit, journey to my spirit." As you climb up, you will pass through an opening or portal and arrive somewhere. A spirit will be standing there.

Walk up and ask, "Are you my spirit? Are you my higher self?" If the answer is yes, extend your hand and meet. If the answer is no, keep looking and repeating, "Journey to my spirit, journey to my spirit," like a mantra because it is your intention.

When you find your spirit, you are then welcome to travel around holding hands. When you are ready to come back, go back to the exact spot where you first met your spirit. Thank them.

Climb back down the golden cord. Make sure you arrive back where you started, with the cord right next to your body and drumming your hands. Invite your traveling consciousness to lie right back down into your body and get settled back in just as you were before your journey.

Stop drumming your hands. This will bring you out of your meditative state.

Now, come back to yourself. Pat yourself down on your limbs and torso and say aloud, "I am here now. I am here now." This will help you ground yourself back into your body and disconnect from the spiritual plane you were visiting. It is important to fully come back to yourself.

Make sure you feel fully present in yourself before going about your day. If you do not, use the grounding exercise in chapter 21, "Grounding into Gaia."

You can journal about your experience.

Your true self is a boundless spiritual being. You are spirit in body.
#joyfulliving101

38. flora fabulous

*Affirmation: "I connect with the world of flora
and experience the bliss of that connection!"*

Everything is alive. Everything has consciousness, including plants. Opening yourself to experience it can up your bliss factor. You can really connect with the beauty of plants in a deeper and more meaningful way. You can feel the interconnection between all life even more when you open your heart to the plants all around you all the time.

Some people have memories of being children and sitting and reading with their back up against a big tree. It felt good there. Safe. And it was, because big trees are steady and strong and their consciousness is supportive and massive. Kids can feel that security and enjoy being close to it.

Others have memories of being shown around their neighbor's rose garden, enchanted. The colors, textures, and smells provided a blissful sensory experience, and the rose consciousness is sweet and refined, almost as if it is playing a lyrical tune. Children can feel these beautiful vibrations easily and respond to them.

Some people have wonderful memories of picking wild strawberries for jam. The plants gave their sweetness with love, and the jam was the best you ever tasted. Children would sing and dream while wandering in the strawberry bramble, not realizing they were connecting with the consciousness of the plants.

The beauty and wisdom of plants is all around you. Start listening!

Exercise: Be a Plant Whisperer

If the weather is inviting to you, go outside now and physically touch plants, trees, soil, etc. Sit with your back against trees or work in the garden. Be with plants and growing flora. Smell flowers and appreciate that they give their sweetness freely, hoping to attract a bee to bless them with pollen and blessing you in the process.

All of those actions will help you connect with the plants surrounding you, whether it be the tree outside your bedroom window, the potted plant in your living room, or the garden in your yard. Start expanding your awareness and connect with the plants you encounter in your day-to-day life—the stand of pine trees you pass every day on your way to work, the vegetables in your salad at dinner, and the grass growing next to the bus stop on a street you frequent. Notice plants, and they will notice you. Give your good wishes to plants, and they will pour forth good wishes to you.

When you connect with a plant, what does it feel like? Is each one different? Do you feel like each one has a personality of sorts or not? Take time to connect with plants. Even saying hi to a tree as you pass by can be a blissful experience if you are open to it.

Flowers, trees, and leaves are all gorgeous expressions of nature's innate joy. Notice the bounty surrounding you.
#joyfulliving101

39. abundance

Affirmation: "I am filled with abundance, gratitude, and love."

You live in an endlessly abundant universe, a domain where everything exists somewhere, somehow. We have all been all things, from one end of the universe to the other. Your true nature, the part of you that connects to the cosmos, is complete and utter bliss. Bliss is the reality of who you really are. It is the sensation we feel when wholeness and pleasure come together in a state of perfection, and one route to tap into this sensation is gratitude.

Being grateful is the magic poultice that heals your wounds. Gratitude is the potent elixir that ignites your bliss. Conscious thankfulness effervesces your soul so that bliss bubbles up. Taking the grateful route to bliss is soul nourishing. It helps you better your life by affirming all the things that you like and want more of in your world. It's easy to be grateful when you see abundance everywhere.

Most discord on the planet comes from fear and lack. Wars, prejudice, and even being judgmental come from fear and lack. Fear is the opposite of love, so love is its remedy.

Lack is the fear of not having enough. It is the opposite of abundance, so feeling abundant and grateful is its remedy. It's simple. Be grateful and feel abundant, and your spirit will become more so. This is true even if you are going through hard times or have in the past. It may not always seem like it, but there are always things to be grateful for.

It's important to let go of the negative, whether in your past or present. If we focus on the negative, pretty soon that is all we can see. But make a conscious choice to be loving and focus on love, and your life will be filled with it. What we put our attention on creates our reality. What gets attention gets done. Our feelings and thoughts are precise magnetic attractors and they also fuel our actions, which create our reality.

So to be surrounded by bliss, be blissful inside. To be abundant, be grateful. To be loved, love others and yourself. Dance your abundant bliss. Combine bliss and abundance and get something very, very special called abun*dance*.

Exercise: Abun*dance* Ritual

Abun*dance* is about bringing your gratefulness and inner emotional abundance to life in a unique, special, sacred dance. It's your own ritual for abundance, and it's powerful.

You can do your abun*dance* daily, weekly, monthly, or even yearly. It is your time to shine, and you can do it solo or in a group. You can try different variations, and it is never the same twice. This might seem silly at first, but dancing and movement to express gratitude is a cross-cultural, ancient tradition. From Native American tribes to Celtic peoples to African and Asian cultures, dancing one's gratitude is a more common practice than you might think. Today you might choose to step out of your comfort zone and try it for a few minutes. Bliss may very well await, but you won't know unless you try.

Clear a space indoors or outdoors. Beautify the area. You might string up garlands of flowers or make colorful signs. Set a jubilant stage. Decide on music. It could be something you play or sing yourself or from a recording of any kind.

Get the people together. It might be just you, you and your pets, or you and your buds. Dress in your finest party outfit or in your ceremonial garb. Start the music and begin to dance. Visualize what you are thankful for as you dance.

See it in your mind and let your surroundings recede while letting your body move however it feels inspired. You might jump up and down. You might roll around on the floor. You might hip-hop dance. Just move organically.

Start speaking or singing aloud about your gratitude. Sing thank you to life. Sing about all your blessings. Dance to punctuate your words. Feel colors as you move and sing. You can close your eyes to tune in to them. Notice them. Be grateful for the colors, the richness, and the dance.

When it feels complete, turn off any recordings and lie on the floor in quiet. Soak in the blissful gratitude vibes. Notice the colors. Feel your insides. Sense your emotions and energy.

How do you feel? After about ten minutes, sit up, journal about your experience, and share with your group if there is one. Before concluding, thank everyone involved, including yourself.

Dance is medicine. Movement is potent.
Empower yourself with it today.
#joyfulliving101

40. Sea of Love

Affirmation: "*I live love in each moment.*
I let love heal me and elevate me to my highest self."

The turquoise water glinted in the sun as the boat cut through the mild chop on the Atlantic. The island of North Bimini faded toward the horizon, and my mind flashed back to images from a dream from the night before: dolphin's eyes and smiles, air bubbles in warm ocean water, the feeling of my heart opening wider and the essence of peace.

Someone on the boat spoke to me, and I responded in kind, making conversation as the boat sped on. On the bow someone yelled, "Dolphins!"

Everyone ran up to the front of the boat. Dolphins were why we were all here on the boat and why we had traveled to the sun-washed islands of the Bahamas in the first place.

We all lay on our bellies on the front of the boat with our heads hanging over the side and watched the dolphins below us effortlessly riding the underwater wave created by the boat's movement through the water. Their enjoyment was palpable, and sometimes one of them would turn on one side and look up at me, making gentle eye contact for a minute. Then it whizzed away out to sea, only to be replaced by a brother or sister from the pod.

"Join our pod," they seemed to beckon.

The dolphins played in the wake of the boat for hours and then it was time for the people to get into the water. In the middle of the Atlantic Ocean the choice to stay or go when we stopped the boat and got into the sea was clearly theirs. They stayed. Cautious at first, they checked us out and swam beneath us.

As we all acclimated to each other, they grew bolder and came closer. Their playful spirit of unconditional love had everyone in a blissful state. I dove with my fins, mask, and snorkel down about fifteen feet. I knew from previous dolphin experiences that they loved when I dove down deeper into their world.

At the bottom of my descent, I hung underwater headfirst. A group of adult dolphins swam from beneath me directly toward me. One of them in the front and center made eye contact with me, telling me, "Relax, we will gently surround you now."

They swam all around me as we made the journey back to the surface together. There were at least five of them all around me, moving, swimming mere centimeters from my body, and almost touching my arms and shoulders but not quite. Each of their eyes lightly held my gaze for a moment until they swam past. The one who led the pack from below gently sidled up in front of me. His beak almost on my forehead, he looked within me and sent me acceptance beyond words. With his gaze and transcendent heart connection, he welcomed me into the pod for all time.

That pod still visits me in dreams from time to time, and I them. We are joined in love. We all share the understanding that love transcends space and time and does not necessarily require physical proximity. We live the knowledge that love is free.

Imagine a world where all the oceans were made of love. Those seas would lap at the shores, saturating the land they touched with the unstoppable power of love. Love is a force of nature that permeates everything in the universe. And you can tap into those endless seas of love and let them spill into your life and transform it.

You can fill your spirit and being with the self-correcting, self-regulating force of ultimate love. It flows in a sparkling stream, and all you need to do is hop in and start swimming.

Join me there now.

Exercise: Floating in Love

The following activity is designed to help you absorb the love coursing through all of nature.

Lie down in a warm, quiet place. Close your eyes and breathe deeply. Let the noise of the day fall away. Envision yourself looking out at a glimmering, pale-pink sea. Stand on the shore and take in the beauty.

Now gently wade in. Feel the pale pink water on your feet. What does it feel like? It's lightly effervescent. Walk in further. Notice it caressing your calves and thighs as you go in deeper.

When you are ready, kick up your heels and allow your legs to float up as you lie on your back in the sea of love. Let the gentle effervescence support you in perfect comfort. Open to the essence of this love water. It is the love that courses through the veins of the divine. Receive it. Allow yourself to be a sponge and soak it in. It is infinite, never-ending.

Sense your heart relaxing, opening. Feel the love water flow into it, swishing in and gently, easily letting any density within wash away. It instantly dissolves in the love water. Breathe deeply and, if you feel ready, dive down into the sea. Swim underwater. You can breathe this water, just like you did as an embryo. Breathe in the love water as you swim in the pale pink, clear sea. What do you feel? What do you sense?

What do you see? There are gentle, completely loving beings in this ocean. They will only approach you if you invite them. Do you see a loving, playful, pink dolphin up ahead? Or a wise, calm, purple whale? If you do, go visit if you'd like. Swim free.

When you are ready, swim back to the surface. Float for a few minutes, soaking in the love. Then swim toward shore. When you are ready, lightly walk out until you are standing on shore looking back out at the sea, just like when you started.

Give thanks to the power of love. Feel the love you just absorbed coursing through you. Step back from the sea and open your eyes when you are ready. Notice the room around you. Pat your arms and legs vigorously and say aloud, "I am here now." Make sure you feel present to yourself before you go about your day. Focus on your five senses to feel rooted in your life.

Your life is awash in waves of love in each moment.
Open your eyes to the currents around you and bathe in the bliss.
#joyfulliving101

41. music to awaken your soul

Affirmation: "*Music enlivens my soul and opens my heart to ever greater levels of bliss and joy.*"

Music is defined as harmonious sounds that produce beauty and stir emotions. That's the amazing thing about music—it expresses emotions. It creates harmony to stir the soul. It ignites things with bliss. Some music can relax you, and some music can jazz you up. Music can inspire people to dance vigorously, rest and fall into a deep sleep, or think about a past emotional moment. Music is powerful!

Music has a unique power to truly stir your soul and heart. And integrating music into your life can bring greater amounts of bliss. You can use music to bring excitement into a dreary day, or you can use music to relax you as you soak in a soothing bubble bath.

To enhance your bliss today, immerse yourself in music! Appreciate the amazing creativity that goes into every kind of music, and experience the bliss that music offers.

Exercise: Music Appreciation

When I was a freshman in high school, I was pleasantly surprised to discover that my music appreciation class was my favorite class of my entire high school experience. It was so much fun to listen to different types of music, enjoy most of them, and notice their gifts. This activity is dedicated to all the music teachers in the world who share the joy of music with their students. (And to that one particular music teacher, up in heaven now, this one's for you!)

Get out your journal and make a list of ten different genres of music. Choose some that you know that you like and some that you haven't heard often. Some fun choices might include bluegrass, ambient, electronica, classical, folk, Celtic, lullabies, chamber music, swing, Latin rap, indie pop, smooth jazz, *kayōkyoku*, opera, doo-wop, ska, rockabilly, calypso, polka, and zydeco.

Listen to a song from one genre. You can do this by using any of the numerous online personalized radio apps available, by searching that genre word online, or by using your own music library.

If you aren't sure where to find a type of music, you can always ask social media. There are usually online groups who love all kinds of niche music and would love to give you recommendations of their favorite songs in the particular genre they appreciate.

Let's say that the first genre on your list is flamenco. Queue up a flamenco song that is new to you or close to new. Listen to the song and write in your journal about how it makes you feel. What do you like about it? Does it inspire bliss?

Go through and do that same process with all other nine genres listed. Look back through your notes and think about which ones you like; pick your top three and circle them. Are these the types of genres you usually listen to?

Look through some more and see if there are others that you usually do not listen to that you ended up enjoying. If you did, then add those to your heavy-rotation repertoire. Pick out genres and types of music that make you feel good. Music is all about opening your heart and feeling emotion. Pick the ones that bring about good emotions and enhance your joy today.

Let music ignite your vivid inner colors
and bring you harmony inside and out.
#joyfulliving101

42. IDENTIFYING POWER

Affirmation: "I am powerful in my love for myself.
My inner essence sparkles with bliss."

You are superhuman. This is because you are special, precious, and a treasure of true beauty. You are amazing! You have endless wonderful qualities. And you have an amazing inner strength and resilience within you. Couple this inner strength and resilience with the truth that anything is possible, and you are the ultimate powerhouse.

You have strength inherently within you. It's deep, amazing strength, and it's the same part of you that is so special. It's also uniquely strong. It's your essence!

Your essence, when properly tapped, can turn you into a superhuman. It's the fuel that gets you exactly where you need to be. It's the clarity that helps you make amazing decisions. It's the inspiration that helps you create beautiful things. Your essence is your inner, special spark that flows throughout your body. A big dose of it lives in your heart center. And it also is strong in your solar plexus, which is often associated with personal power. Your essence is that special, individuated part of you that is uniquely you. It's interwoven with your overall chi or energy, and it's in every cell and synapse of your being. Your essence is beautiful—tap into it today!

Exercise: Essential Essence

In this activity you're going to practice tapping into your power center in order to recharge your creativity, optimism, love, and bliss. This is a great way to connect with your individual essence. Your solar plexus offers an easy way to connect with that part of your being.

Find a quiet place to sit and be still. Take a few minutes to relax your mind and heart. Feel the air moving in and out of your body. Breathe deeply.

As you relax, place your hands on your solar plexus, above your belly button and below your chest. Feel that area. Feel the energy there. Feel the power there. This is your power center, where your unique and powerful essence lives.

Feel your consciousness go into that space. Pay attention to how it feels there. Let yourself go deep within it. Imagine you're standing there in your own solar plexus. What does it feel like? What does it look like? What does it sound and smell like? Notice the colors. Feel the power there. Feel the spark within you and immerse yourself in it. Tap into this essence and let it fuel you. Let it fuel your creative fire. Let it fuel your heart and its ability to love. Let your spark fuel your decisive optimism and your actions.

As you sit with the spark within you, think of the word "bliss." Send your intention to live a strong, powerful, blissful life, and run it through your solar plexus, where it will get powered up. Radiate it out through your body and into the world. This will draw powerful bliss right back to you. Say thank you to your divine essence, and say yes to the bliss you already contain. You are powerful! You are superhuman! Live it!

Your inner essence can innovate and inspire. Harness that dynamism and embrace the positive change you can create. #joyfulliving101

43. angels all around for peaceful sleep

Affirmation: "*I allow myself to rest deeply and be rejuvenated,
trusting the love of the angels to support
and hold me for my highest good.*"

We are surrounded by helping spirits all the time. These beings are respectful, honoring, and totally benevolent. The angels are a special group of these beings. We can ask the angels for help with anything.

Peaceful sleep is essential to our health and well-being. We can ask the angels to help with this. They are happy to assist us and care about our well-being and happiness.

In the following section, we will work specifically with Archangel Michael. You may or may not have heard of him. He is a being who cares for all of humanity with clear, nonjudgmental, unconditional love. He is happy to assist us in feeling safe and protected, and that is one of his many specialties.

Some of his other interests include spreading the essence of love through as many light particles as possible and spending time with other beings who are also in a state of love and bliss.

Exercise: Invoke Archangel Michael and Seal Your Space

The invocation of Archangel Michael is useful for protection and to feel extra secure throughout daily life, in crowds, in challenging situations, or while sleeping. This is great to say before bed, and you can post it on the wall or nightstand as a soothing poster. Repeat the invocation aloud or internally and feel the atoms surrounding you being infused with Archangel Michael's loving presence.

The Invocation of Archangel Michael

Archangel Michael before me
Archangel Michael behind me
Archangel Michael to the left of me
Archangel Michael to the right of me
Archangel Michael above me
Archangel Michael below me
Archangel Michael is here on earth
I am love, protected
I am love, protected
I am love, protected
It is done

Exercise: Seal Up

Another helpful before-sleep ritual is sealing up your energy. Sometimes we are very open mentally, even while we sleep. We need to rest, and that openness can be distracting and get distorted while we are trying to process our subconscious emotions through dreams. Here is a way to quiet some of the outside energy in the area where we are sleeping. Repeat these words aloud or internally: "I seal and protect all openings in my energetic and physical bodies in all dimensions and realities as needed for my highest good and the highest good of all life for all time. I own my space, and only that which is of the light may enter. It is done."

At the same time, imagine your attention at the top of a bubble extending out around your body three feet in all directions. Picture a rush of energy or wind circling out around the bubble and spiraling down around it, eventually reaching the bottom and going into the earth below you. This wind or energy will touch every inch of the bubble in transit to the earth.

You can now relax in your space and feel secure. These two processes are wonderful to do each night before bed.

Angels are all around us every day.
Notice them and realize the benevolence of life.
#joyfulliving101

44. comfort and joy

Affirmation: "I use healthy joy and comfort to set off my brain chemicals of bliss for my highest good."

Part of finding your bliss is developing a sense of comfort and joy in your daily life. You can give yourself comfort by prioritizing your restoration and rejuvenation. You can soak in mineral baths. You can fill your home with soft-colored wildflowers. You can meditate. You can collect shells. You can discover new gentle places. You can create bliss and quiet in your life by setting aside time to meditate or do yoga. You can give yourself the chance to dream and be friendly with your imagination. You can surround yourself with color and mystical, enchanting pictures and items that will comfort you, like images of fairies, flowers, or tranquil clouds. There are endless possibilities to creating comfort in your life if you make it a priority. You will be giving yourself the message that you are loved and cared for and that your comfort matters. And in doing so, you will give yourself the freedom to be replenished on a continual basis, which allows you to feel more and more joy.

Comfort and joy combined create true bliss. When you put those two ingredients together, you ignite endless, abundant experiences of bliss. Who wouldn't want that?

Exercise: Experience Comfort and Joy

We are going to define what really embodies these two important feelings for you so that you can make them critical ingredients in your life. They are inseparable and essential to feeling amazing and experiencing bliss.

Let's begin with comfort. Brainstorm in your journal about some times when you have felt deeply comforted. During these times, you felt sensory enjoyment and relaxation. Really remember what this feeling was like. What were you doing? Were you at a spa soaking in the fizzy mineral bath? Were you lying on a sun-drenched beach with a light breeze? Were you floating on a raft in the middle of a glistening lake at sunset? Were you wrapped up in the softest blanket on a puffy featherbed? Were you eating sweet, sensual honey and listening to gorgeous music?

Really remember and experience what that felt like and write it down. Ask yourself what are some other ways you might feel that same feeling. What are some things you could do or situations you could put yourself in to feel deep, sensory comfort and relaxation? Write those down.

Do the same exercise about when you felt soaring joy. Think about when you felt that pleasurable feeling last and about the peak moments. What were you doing? Were you standing on a surfboard for the first time, shooting over the water? Were you looking through a telescope at a bright moon? Had you just climbed your favorite tree and you were looking over your neighborhood? Were you rollerblading down a huge hill, flying over the pavement? Were you dancing onstage to a favorite song?

Really bring yourself back to that feeling. Brainstorm some other ways that you might feel that same feeling. Write them down in your journal.

Pick your top idea for each feeling. It is your job to schedule both of these experiences for yourself in the next ten days. When you do them, really let yourself be one hundred percent present to how they feel. Did they meet your expectations? Were they different from what you imagined? Let yourself feel amazing. Let yourself feel deeply comforting and joyful bliss. Give yourself these pleasurable experiences to raise your mood and vibration and to enhance your bliss.

Comfort, joy, and love are key ingredients to a rich,
pleasurable life. Prize them.
#joyfulliving101

45. Live for today

Affirmation: "*I embrace now—this moment—
with my whole being.*"

What do you think is the purpose of life? Really give it some thought for a moment. There is no correct answer, and each person's answer will be highly individual. Do we all have the exact same purpose, or are the reasons we are here as varied as our diverse beauty? Does the purpose of life involve joy or bliss for you? Odds are it does in some form, whether it's spiritual joy, the heart-joy of connecting with family, or the joy of accomplishing tasks and achieving goals.

Finding your bliss is an inside job, and there is no time to waste. Today could be your last day to really live. This isn't meant to be sad or scary. Today, you are here! There is so much to experience, and it's a gift to have the opportunity. Don't waste a minute.

In 2007, I was driving slowly and safely down an almost-clear road in winter. It wasn't slippery after the snowstorm the night before, and it was just a normal morning. An ordinary day like any other was getting started as I headed to work.

Suddenly, I hit a patch of black ice, and my car rolled down a hill. After what seemed like minutes, I landed abruptly on a tree. I crawled out of the broken driver's side window as I grabbed my purse, shards of glass falling to the ground from my hair and clothes. I was okay. I was alive. And what stuck with me was the feeling of peace I felt as I rolled down that hill on spin cycle. I was present and living for today. It further strengthened my belief that we can choose to be present and conscious in our lives and that if we do, our lives will align with our highest purpose. And then, whenever we exit this reality, we will be at peace.

Exercise: Your Prime Directive

If you were to live for today, what would you do? To figure that out, you must identify what is important to you. Answer the following questions to find out:

+ Who are you in your heart?
+ What ignites passionate interest in you? What lights up your spirit?
+ Where are you going in life? What drives you?
+ What feelings do you seek in your life?
+ What do you fear?
+ What do you hope for?
+ What is your wish?

- What do you offer to life?
- What do you need to be happy?
- What brings you joy?

Take some time to really reflect on your answers. Use them to identify your prime directive. What drives you at your core? What fuels your actions, thoughts, and decisions?

Whatever drives you is what you must construct your life around. If it's connecting with others, then your life must be filled with sweet connection. If it is spiritual reflection and solitude, then you must make that a priority. If you are fueled by time in nature, then those moments must become a top consideration.

Living for today means identifying your bliss and experiencing it now. Because *now* is the only moment that truly exists. Right now. Everything else is a whisper, but now is essential. And all moments, future and past, are contained in this one. All things are simultaneous. Living for today is choosing bliss in each moment, on the days with your favorite activities and even when you are grocery shopping, doing laundry, carpooling, or working at a restaurant. Connectors can smile and share goodwill with whomever they meet, whether they're doing errands or consciously connecting. The spiritual reflector can see the divine beauty in the carpool, the serenity of doing laundry, and the exchange of energy while working at a restaurant. The nature enthusiast can appreciate nature on the way to the grocery store and even in selecting produce to nourish their family.

Live for today and find the joy in each moment. Be present to this day and savor it.

In choosing consciousness, we gift ourselves with presence.
#joyfulliving101

46. you are wired for joy

Affirmation: "*I am wired to live joy in all ways.*
I let my being be healed and tended by the high vibration of joy.
My life is optimized for boundless joy."

You are made to be joyful. Your body wants to find comfort and pleasure. Your heart wants to find love and healthy connection. Your mind wants to find understanding and enjoyment. Your spirit wants to feel the divine spark of delight. All these parts of you are seeking. They are striving to grow, to learn, to create a happy world for you.

Exuberance is within you. You can source your inner being from it. And you can circulate it through your body as a healing and enlivening force. Begin to think of joy not only as a feeling or emotion but also as a type of energy. Like electricity, it flows through things that best conduct it. Your body is the optimum conductor for joy!

It is time for a tune-up to turn up the volume and optimize your joy receptors. It is time for an upgrade so you can feel elation more deeply and amplify its energy in your life and body.

Exercise: Upgrade Your Wiring

To update your joy system, you can experience the process below. Follow along and the directions will take you through the whole rewire. This will help you be more energetically available to feeling delight and experiencing deep happiness. In turn, your health and well-being will be enhanced, and your quality of life will raise. We will start with your mind and then work with your body.

Mind

This exercise for the mind is something I use with my medical intuitive clients. It may seem a little bit abstract. Techniques like this one that use visualization of a shape and then moving and changing it have created healing and caused positive shifts in many of my clients over the years. Similar things are done in hypnotherapy.

I believe you can rewire your brain on an energetic level using the visualization we are about to do. There has not been a lot of scientific study around these types of activities thus far, but I am sharing with you what has worked for many people I have worked with over the last fifteen years.

Take a moment to breathe deeply and calm your mind and body. Place your tongue on the roof of your mouth, resting it comfortably just behind your front teeth. In yoga and *chi gong* this is known to help you be more relaxed and focused. In my medical intuitive practice, I have observed that it helps the two sides of the brain work together more easily. Close your eyes for a moment and picture a three-dimensional shape before you. Just let the first thing that comes to mind be there. Notice its color, size, and texture.

Envision the shape beginning to spin. See it get going very fast. Let your tongue relax now. Say the word "joy" aloud while aiming the sound into the center of the shape. Sound is powerful and holds vibration strongly. Keep repeating it while the shape changes and discharges energy. When it stops spinning, you can stop saying "joy."

Envision the shape again. Has it changed? Is it a different shape, color, or texture? Do you hear, smell, or taste anything associated with it? It will dissolve in a moment. Strange as it may seem, that exercise rewired your brain for joy. Now it's time for your body.

Body

Rub your palms together vigorously. With each rub, say the word "joy" aloud. Do this for a minute or two. When it is complete, your hands naturally will slow and stop.

Next, place your fingertips together like a steeple—each thumb to thumb, pointer finger to pointer finger, etc. Pull them apart and bring them together back four times, saying "joy" once each time. Drop your hands, and state aloud, "I now allow my body, mind, heart, and spirit to reconfigure for optimum joy experiences in my life and for my best health. I enact this change for the highest good of all life and in accordance with universal natural law. It is done."

Say aloud, "Proper universal alignment. Proper universal alignment. Proper universal alignment." This is a potent phrase that I have used with my medical intuitive clients for the last six years. I have observed that it realigns the body, mind, and spirit with what is for the highest good for the person who says it. Sometimes people feel their spines straighten and their minds clear. Sometimes the change is subtle and quiet, just a whisper of greater well-being.

You're done! You are rewired for joy. Your body responds to this process because it wants to be lined up with joy, and now it is.

We are all wired to experience boundless joy and lavish bliss.
#joyfulliving101

47. waves of welcome

*Affirmation: "I give and accept waves of welcome.
I attract wonderful, like-minded friends who enrich my life."*

On Twitter, #WOW can mean "waves of welcome." It's used to greet new friends in the Twitterverse. The spirit of waves of welcome is one of friendliness and openness. Meeting new people can enrich your life. And all of your close friends were once strangers. Friendliness and sharing are the ingredients that create friendships.

Extend waves of welcome to people you meet, and be open to heart connections. They happen all the time. An open heart is free and trusting yet strong and empowered. You can believe in the goodness in the world. You can trust your radar and heart. You know what is best for you. Trust yourself.

Exercise: Friendly Heart

In this exercise we will explore if you want to allow yourself to have a friendly heart. Do you encounter any resistance? Are you afraid of getting hurt, seeming weak, losing something, losing your edge, being duped?

Someday, you will have to release your fears and trust the wisdom of your heart. Why not make it today? If you do, you will make more space in your heart for love and joy.

Your heart is wise and capable of more than your mind. Your mind is limited in that it accounts for knowledge but not emotion. Your heart is limitless. Place your bets on the heart.

If you want to have a friendly heart, try this:

Bring your attention to the center of your chest. Feel the energy there. Envision it glowing. Let your heart energy radiate. Just feel it and notice if it pulses or feels warm. Your attention helps it radiate.

Ask your heart if it wants to open. Listen for its answer. You may feel it emotionally or sensorially. Visualize your heart responding and opening. If it is apprehensive, ask it why. What fears come up? Breathe into them and open yourself to love. Feel the breath go into the center of your chest. Keep breathing deeply into your heart, and simultaneously try to let yourself relax. Relaxing is opening.

Now say aloud, "I choose to open my heart. I draw heart friends to me for my highest good. I allow my life to be enriched."

Breath is the door to the heart and soul.
It moves chi and energizes cells.
#joyfulliving101

48. balancing the masculine and feminine sides

Affirmation: "*My sacred twins live in blissful harmony, and I am integrated.*"

Your sacred twins symbolize your masculine and feminine sides. Everyone has these aspects of the self. You want your sacred twins to be in harmony. You want them to be good buddies. This fosters greater integration of your spirit and emotions, and that makes your human experience more positive and efficient. This concept began as an ancient shamanic tradition from the Yucatán Peninsula in Mexico.

You are going to meet your sacred twins. Your job will be to facilitate a positive and joyful experience for each one. They may be cooperative and excited to see you and each other, or they may have some things to work out. You can handle it! You are perfectly equipped to help them get to know each other if they haven't met. And you're also the perfect consciousness to assist them in deepening and bettering their relationship.

The masculine and feminine labels are only to describe the polarity and relationship between those aspects of the self. In many, they will appear as the gender stated, but there is no constraint to that. Different people's sacred twins show up in different ways. All manifestations are beautiful.

Your masculine side is usually the right side of your body and left side of your brain. It is responsible for logical, rational thinking. It likes lists, efficiency, security, and wise action. Masculine is active.

Your feminine side is usually the left side of your body and right side of your brain. It is responsible for your creativity and out-of-the-box thinking. It likes beauty, expression, and flowing movement. Feminine is receptive.

Exercise: Meet Your Sacred Twins

In order to unite the masculine and feminine sides of your body energetically and help the left and right hemispheres of your brain work together more cooperatively, you can meet your sacred twins and help them become a more unified team. This shamanic technique will bring you greater wellness and cohesion of your spirit.

Lie down and relax your mind and body for a few minutes. Repeat the word "bliss" over and over in your mind. Let your thoughts converge on that word. Let it permeate you. Bliss. It's your goal. It's happiness, contentment, pleasure, peace, uplift, and positivity. Be bliss for a few minutes by saying the word to yourself. When you repeat a word over and over, its essence gets programmed into the cells of your body.

Now, say aloud, "I now choose to meet my sacred twins for my highest good and the highest good of all life. I ask that this meeting be gentle, pleasant, and mutually beneficial for all aspects of myself involved. I thank my sacred twins for showing up to meet me consciously today. I appreciate you both equally."

Close your eyes and sink into your consciousness. Cross your hands over the center of your chest. Envision a door, open it, and walk through. See yourself entering an appropriately appointed room, the environment fitting you. It is the center of the temple of your heart. Feel yourself walk into the center of the room. From your right, one sacred twin will walk out to meet you now.

From the left, the other will emerge and join you. Outstretch your hands and all hold hands in a circle. Introduce yourself. Allow them to also introduce themselves. Ask them if they need anything from you to make their lives and jobs easier. Listen.

Tell them which of those things you can do. Invite them to dialogue. Listen to the discourse and offer help or mediation as needed. When that is complete and they are in harmony, invite a group hug.

Give them both flowers that you easily conjure from your hands. Thank them. Receive any gifts they may offer. Tell them they can meet you in the dreamtime whenever they want or ask you to come visit again.

Hug again and then exit through the door, closing it firmly but gently. Open your eyes and drink a full glass of water to hydrate and integrate. Journal about your experience.

Integration happens when all parts of your being are in harmony. #joyfulliving101

49. fairy finding

Affirmation: "I honor and love the fairy folk and am excited to keep getting to know them for the rest of my life!"

Another word for fairy is elemental. Elementals are involved with almost every facet of existence. These beings shape the landscape of wild terrain. They cheer us on as we plant our gardens and advise us with gentle whispers where to place seeds and bulbs. These beings teach us how to walk softly on the planet.

I believe elementals also move the stars that orbit the center of galaxies. They encourage the energy that comprises gravity, centripetal force, and other forces of nature. Frequently, elementals lovingly tend and support something in the natural world, whether a flower, a tree, a star, or a stone. The elementals of gravity may sound extra cosmic to some people. In my personal experience and the happenings of many clients over the years, this has been truth. An important thing to remember is that spiritual experiences are unique for every individual. Forces in the spirit world may seem real for some and not for others. The truth is that your beliefs and focus create your reality. Every moment provides an opportunity to expand your view and thinking. The result is often a new sense of joy and a more open heart.

Play is the essence of fairy life. Fairy play can change lives and universes. It can enliven a plant, brighten a flower, and midwife a supernova explosion.

The other essence of fairy energy and elemental life is change. Change is one of the constants in the universe. Change does not stop. Lack of change, also known as stagnation, creates a vacuum energetically. And nature does everything it can to fill a vacuum; in the case of fairy energy, it does so with change.

Change is a great ally to the fae (another name for the fairy folk). The fae dance with change and harness its power to manifest living miracles of creation constantly. For the fae, change is one of the constants they depend on. The other is love.

Fairies have a deep, abiding sense of love. Love, for the fae, is unencumbered. It is universal life and light. It is string-free. It just is. Love is the nature of true reality and divine presence. Love is energy, power, and electricity. Fairies and elementals of all kinds harness love to manifest change. Love and change are interwoven in the fae realm and throughout the universe.

Exercise: Witness Beauty with a Fairy Friend

Sit outside near some flowers, plants, or trees that you like. You can do this during any season. Just find some plants that you feel are speaking to you. This can be in your yard, in a park, in a forest, or by a lake or the ocean. Leave your cell phone off or away from you.

Look around and appreciate the beauty surrounding you. Spend some time just relaxing and acclimating to the gentler pace of nature. It's not overstimulating. It's balanced and peaceful. Feel that. Close your eyes and notice the smells around you. Do you smell the flowers? Let your thoughts slow down. Relax your mind. Allow your heart to open.

Say aloud, "Fairy folk, fairy folk, fairy folk, come visit me and let me see you. I come to you in only love and light." You could also sing this, since fairies love music. You have to call them aloud. You can whisper it if you'd like.

Feel them gather. Open your eyes and see if you sense or know that they are there, right in front of you. They may be like little moving sparkles.

If you sense them, say hello (or, even better, lyrically sing it). Commune with them. Connect with them. Open your heart and mind to their messages. Enjoy your time together. Thank them when you are finished, and journal your experiences afterward.

The fairy folk are all around! Start noticing their beauty, and feel blissful connection with them! To encourage them to interact with you more often, you can build a fairy home in a corner of your yard or garden. Find natural materials such as leaves, twigs, feathers, or pretty pebbles, and construct something that you find beautiful and would give the fairies someplace to manifest when you are seeking to communicate with them. They may also choose to rest there at other times, blessing your garden with their presence.

Fairy magic is present in every ray of sunlight and each joyful moment. Embrace the living essence of nature.
#joyfulliving101

50. ancestral healing

Affirmation: "I keep the light and love from my ancestors and let go of the rest."

The world is changing rapidly. A global homogenization is happening. Beautiful races of every color are intermingling like never before. Now more than ever, it is very apparent how intertwined we all are.

People are tracing their ancestry and discovering distant relatives all across the world. People are reconnecting with lost heritages. The global reality is moving closer and closer to acceptance and embracing. It may take a while for the entire world to catch up, but overall progress toward love and equality marches on.

What a perfect time to clean up any density or old energy related to our ancestry and step into greater bliss! The more density we dissolve, the more space we make for joy, light, bliss, and goodness. Own your ancestry, whether you know the complete picture of it or not. Embrace yourself and your hundreds of thousands of ancestors, going all the way back to the beginning of humanity. You are diverse and ancient! Heal and celebrate who you are.

Exercise: Ancestral Balancing and Harmony Process

The purpose of this activity is to connect with your ancestral spirits and dissolve as much density as possible from your being in order to allow healing and balance.

Say aloud, "I would now like to do the Ancestral Balancing and Harmony Process." This calls in the beings of light who can support you in this activity. Close your eyes. Place your tongue on the roof of your mouth right behind your front teeth. Doing this is thought to help the two sides of your brain work in greater harmony. It is also known to increase focus and help you meditate.

Above your head, envision a revolving form or shape. It will be different for everyone. This is a medical intuitive technique that lets you bring energy or thought into temporary form so that you can change it or balance it. Experience it by noticing how it feels to you. Do you notice a color or scent with it? Sense into the form by letting your attention merge with it. Disengage your mind as much as possible, and notice if it has a sound or emotion associated with it. This gives sensory insight into parts of your ancestral lineage outside of the mind and thoughts.

Say aloud, "I receive all blessings and love for the highest good from my ancestors. I release with love all that does not serve me and my highest good from my ancestors for all time. So be it. It is done."

Bring your attention back from the energetic form above your head. How does the form feel now? It may have changed and may continue to evolve and change. Say aloud, "Thank you for the gifts and healing of this process and to all the helpers involved. I am grateful and accept bliss and joy as they now fill me."

This is a very nonlinear process and creates a change in the body and the brain that is beyond conventional explanation. It is not intended to engage the mind too much. Sometimes thinking doesn't work, so we try something a little different. This is an opportunity to relax the mind and let the somatic body be balanced. The somatic body is the body and mind. It is the source of intelligence contained in your body and is intrinsically intertwined with your nervous system. This exercise is one of many proprietary techniques that I have created over fifteen years as a medical intuitive working with clients worldwide, and I share it with you because it has worked for many clients over the years.

We can all receive the gifts of our unique ancestry
and harness them to forge a path of joy and healing.
#joyfulliving101

51. stress and anxiety

Affirmation: "*I make time for joy every day.*"

Stress is an epidemic in our culture. Every day, people all over the world experience stress in myriad forms—everything from financial and relationship stress to survival stress. Weathering the storm again and again comes from within. If your heart is filled with love, joy, bliss, and happiness, you can let that carry you through the tougher times. Let that optimistic fuel help you navigate life's ups and downs. But what if you don't feel joyful in your heart all the time? What should you do? It sounds great in theory, but how do you practice it? It is very simple: you fake it till you make it.

Consciously commit to cultivating a happy heart. Find bliss wherever you can. Make it your mission to strengthen yourself—not in a bodybuilding way nor by being a tough cookie, but in a deeper way. Strengthen yourself in a way that focuses on love, joy, and the internal wellspring of good feelings that you possess. Everybody has that. It's just a matter of discovering and uncovering it.

Some ways that you can strengthen your joyful heart, even in times of strife, are committing to joy every day, journaling something joyful every day, setting up fun outings for yourself, calling a friend and watching a hysterically funny comedy while on the phone together, and having a party! Or do something outrageous like take up an activity you've always been too nervous to do before. Spend time with positive, loving people; reach out for connection. Be sure to make time for whatever hobbies bring you joy.

Even in troubled times, those who prioritize balance feel the best. You can be present for yourself or someone else, but also give yourself time to find joy, even if it's just for a few minutes every day. And when you are not in the stressful situation, don't focus on it. Instead, choose to do something joyful. Choose to connect with your happy heart every day. When you do this, you dramatically decrease your propensity for anxiety. Anxiety disorder diagnoses are steadily on the rise. Give yourself the chance to feel as good as you can by giving yourself a daily prescription of joy. And be sure to seek help when you need it.

Exercise: Be Happy Every Day

Now it's time to start filling up with that optimistic fuel I mentioned earlier.

Take out your journal and get ready to make a list. Title your list "Things I Can Do for a Jolt of Happiness." Number the lines one through twenty and start brainstorming things you can do to bring yourself happiness, one per line.

When you reach number ten, stand, jump up, and give a cheer to celebrate reaching the halfway point and to do something physically enlivening. By acting out a feeling with your body and by using your voice, you can generate the feeling within you. This is a way you can influence your own emotions. Keep brainstorming until you reach the bottom of the list.

This will get you started. Every day pick one of these things and enact it, or every day come up with something else to bring yourself joy and happiness. The joy experience can take five minutes or five hours—your choice. But to really not worry and be happy, you must prize happiness and schedule time for joy amid the hectic world in which we live.

Making the effort to experience daily joy is a powerful mood enhancer. Find your bliss today!
#joyfulliving101

52. COLLAGE YOUR HEART

Affirmation: "*My collage opens my heart to endless joy.
I am an artist!*"

Creative endeavors are an amazing way to express your emotions. Creating something—anything, really—can help you process a difficult emotion or integrate past experiences for your highest good. Every time you process or integrate something that was left emotionally unfinished, you make more room in your heart for bliss. You create space for goodness by letting go of what no longer serves you.

Certain things in your life inspire attachment. Some of those things are great. It is human and healthy to feel attached to those that we love. Love is part of the beautiful human experience of having a heart and being present in a body for a period of time.

Feeling attached to the types of experiences you want to have is also natural. As humans, we are propelled by an intricate system of chemicals to seek what feels good. And we are rewarded when we do that with powerful feel-good chemicals. This is the reality of how our bodies are built.

You can harness these realities of love, attachment, and pleasure seeking and use them to your advantage to create a life that you enjoy. You can choose to appreciate the experience of being a human with a delightful array of senses and an opportunity to share love and emotion in this temporary world of duality. You can create bliss in your life. It is actually your job to create your own paradise on earth. It is your personal responsibility to craft your best life. You can experience peak moments and peak living by cultivating bliss, love, and soaring joy.

Creating art also helps you let go of the old to make room for the new. Without even having to consciously think about old wounds or traumas, you can let them go by harnessing your own creativity. This might happen through a painting with pieces of fabric pasted into it, symbolizing the patches that have covered someone's wounds for so long. Sometimes simply by creating that art, the artist is able to let those patches go and let those wounds permanently heal. Healing is alchemical. It's energetic, emotional, and complex. And creativity can sometimes bypass the mind and get into the deep subconscious to cause powerful healing and dramatically increase well-being.

Exercise: Heart Harmony Collage

Today, you are going to create a heart collage on your choice of medium. You might want to do it on a canvas and use decoupage glue to adhere the pictures to your collage. You might also want to do it on construction paper or create a poster board in the shape of a heart. What would be fun? What would you like to put your collage on?

Get that surface ready. Gather your glue, tape, or whatever you want to use to adhere things to your collage. Keep some markers or colored pencils handy. And don't forget the scissors!

Next get some magazines, old picture books, newspapers, brochures, and anything you'd like to cut up and use in your collage. You might cut one word out of an entire magazine; that is okay. You can also print out photographs and use those. Anything goes. You could put a favorite picture of yourself smack dab in the middle!

Take some time and think about your heart. Feel your heart and then begin to flip through all of your collage materials. Cut out anything that stands out for you, be it pictures, words, or anything else. Think about your heart and how you want it to feel. Think about all the good feelings you want to feel. You can also think about your life goals and desires. You can include anything that evokes any of these things. Collages are poetic. They don't always have to be literal and make total sense. You are simply creating beauty.

After you've gathered a bunch of beautiful things to affix to your surface, go for it! Arrange everything in a pleasing manner and glue it on.

Look at your collage and use your colored pencils or markers to write any words or draw any pictures that you want to include. Of course, because this book is all about enhancing your bliss, I suggest you add "bliss" in big, bold, delightful letters—because who doesn't want to have a blissful heart?

When you're finished, gaze at your collage. Appreciate the beauty you created. Enjoy this visual representation of your inner self. It is powerful to see what is within you beautifully expressed in art. Let yourself feel empowered and blissful that you created such a gorgeous piece of art. You are awesome!

Life is like a collage. Its individual pieces are arranged to create harmony. Appreciate the artwork of your life.
#joyfulliving101

53. DRINK from the well of self-Love

*Affirmation: "I let my love for myself grow infinitely.
I understand that loving myself is emotionally healthy
and necessary to my well-being."*

You have an endless well of love within you. It is completely infinite. To truly experience love with another person, you must first have complete, utter, full love for yourself. You must dip yourself in the well of true self-love. You must cultivate self-love relentlessly to create your best life. It's a daily process. You must make the commitment and conscious effort every day to be kind and loving to yourself. You must do this to create a blissful life. It's necessary.

Turn down the volume on your negative self-talk and turn up the volume on your bliss. Speak to yourself with the words of love. Say and think only positive, loving, and accepting words to yourself and about yourself. Can you commit to that? Your cells believe what you tell them. If you tell them, "I am an amazing being of love and light doing my very best every day, and I love myself," you will flourish. You have to choose to commit to loving yourself.

Say the following aloud: "I allow myself to be totally supported in all I do. I am buoyed by love and know I am enfolded in a mantle of pure support for all time. The whole universe conspires to support me, and I am grateful."

Exercise: Quench Your Thirst for Self-Love

The purpose of this activity is to allow you to begin to experience self-love. Once you truly love yourself, you can share your love more fully with others.

Lie down and quietly rest. Relax your body, mind, and heart. Let your spirit be unbounded. Close your eyes and picture that you are lying on the shore of a beautiful body of water. It's like a small pond or spring bubbling up in the middle of a gorgeous landscape.

What does your landscape look like? Is it a seaside hot spring? Is it a fresh forest glade with a spring bubbling up? Is it a gorgeous desert oasis with a fresh, life-giving well at its center? With your eyes closed imagine yourself looking around and taking in the landscape. Notice the sights, smells, and sounds.

Bring your attention to this spring or well next to you. Imagine that you dip your hand into it. Feel what the texture of the liquid feels like. Is it cool, fresh water? Is it foam-like bubbles? Is it effervescing, fizzy water? Is it the softest water you've ever felt? Absorb it through your hand.

Envision yourself reaching your hand in and scooping some of this water out of the spring and tasting it. What does it taste like? As you drink it down, what does it feel like? This is your well of self-love. Take another drink. And another. Drink your fill.

Now you may just want to rest on the shore and absorb the self-love. If you'd like, you can wade into the spring, float, and absorb self-love into every pore. When you're ready, come back out and see yourself lying on that edge of the spring feeling relaxed, loving yourself.

When it feels right, bring your attention back to your physical body in the room where you are actually lying. Run your hands up and down your arms and legs. Do it vigorously to bring sensation into them and say aloud, "I'm here now. I'm present."

Open your eyes when you're ready. Make sure you feel totally present to yourself. You can rub the bottoms of your feet vigorously to help bring you back completely. Then go about your day filled with self-love.

When we fill our hearts with self-love,
we kindle sparks of compassion all around us.
#joyfulliving101

54. SPIRIT WRITING

Affirmation: "I am loved and held by a benevolent universe of love and bliss for all time."

Part of feeling blissful is knowing that we are not alone. We have friends and family to care about how we are doing. Most of these people are alive, and some may not be. There is also an amazing array of spirit helpers all around us all of the time. Depending on our beliefs we might call them different things, like guides, angels, fairies, muses, *dakini*, ascended masters, etc.

These helpers are available to send us love and be present to us in good times and bad. We can sometimes sense them. Whether we know it or not, our life guides are there all the time. These guides have been with us since birth and will be with us until we transition from this life to our next phase of existence. They give us privacy whenever appropriate, but they are never far. You can connect with them anytime you want. Learn how now!

Exercise: Spirit Writing with Your Life Guides and Higher Self

Get a notebook or journal ready with a pen nearby. It's nice to have one journal dedicated to your spiritual journey. In this exercise you will connect with your higher self and one or more life guides.

Get settled in a spot where you can be relaxed and comfortable with your journal in your lap. Close your eyes for a moment and breathe deeply, quieting your mind. Let go of any expectations about this activity and just relax. Simply allow yourself to relax. You don't have to do anything: just let go.

Say aloud, "I connect with my higher self in a space of joy and bliss." Take a moment to feel that connection establish. Simply notice.

Now state aloud, "I ask that all that transpires in this spirit writing session be for the very highest good of all life and in accordance with universal natural law, helping all and harming none. I ask that I be protected fully during this process and now invite my most highly vibrational life guides to connect with me via my higher self."

Sit for a moment with your eyes closed and let this all sink in. Feel the guides around you. Bring your hands out in front of you, palms up at about waist level. This should be comfortable to hold for a few minutes, and if it is not, just adjust accordingly. When you are ready, say aloud, "I invite one of my life guides, approved by my higher self, to connect with me now by hovering her or his spirit hands over my hands so we are almost palm to palm."

Sit and sense for a few minutes. Connect with your guide. Introduce yourself with words either in your mind or aloud.

Listen with your spirit senses for their answer when they introduce themselves.

Tell them you would like to spirit write with them and pick up your pen. Close your eyes partway and let your pen start to move. Just let your mind recede and your pen flow. You may write paragraphs, draw, or just write fragments and words. All of it is fine. Keep going until it slows and ceases.

Thank your life guide and say aloud, "I now disconnect from my life guides within this spirit writing session and return to a clear, clean state of high-vibrational being. I leave this session energized and enhanced, and so does my guide. It is done."

Now, rub your arms and legs vigorously. Make sure you feel fully present to yourself. Also, as you go about your daily activities, take a moment from time to time to remember all the helpers all around you. You are never alone.

Loving spirits are with you every step of the way, cheering you on and offering help when they can. You are never alone.
#joyfulliving101

55. do what feels good

Affirmation: "*I effortlessly let go of my density and dance forward into infinite bliss.*"

Sometimes, seeking joy is the simple act of doing what feels good. When you allow yourself to just be you. When you allow yourself to be immersed in the feelings of freedom and celebration and vitality, you can find your true passion.

Doing what feels good is essential to having a high-quality life. You need to feel pleasure on a very regular basis to keep your mood up. This is how you get the feel-good chemicals that keep you feeling positive about life. We can harness the way our bodies work and create a life that is more consistently enjoyable and positive.

You can find a holistic way of positive living that works for you and is in line with your authentic, true self. It's about knowing that you are a fresh soul, that you are a treasure, and that you deserve ecstasy and light.

You deserve to feel good! And you are responsible for creating a life where that happens every day, many times per day. If you choose to do that, you can dare to come alive. You can discover what it means to be truly happy and to live in the moment. You can live with a new sense of vividness. And you can also experience greater ease and great freedom. You will be inundated with innovative ideas when you do this and you will be radiating and renewing in a luxurious flow of ultimate bliss.

This is the way that life is truly meant to be: blissful and steeped in feelings of sublime enjoyment. You can experience that healthy, kind, loving way of being that enhances you and your planet.

Can you commit to feeling good every day? Can you commit to that and embrace the freedom of feeling good every hour? Can you wrap your mind around the truth that you are unlimited and you can feel good in every moment of your entire life? You are in charge of your experiences and empowered to generate happiness in your life.

Exercise: How to Feel Good

To feel good, you have to jump into a vibration of the positive. You have to choose to be abundant in joy. You have to focus on your true reality of dazzling freedom. You have to make a choice to sparkle and let go of your fears.

The only things that stop you from feeling amazing one hundred percent of the time are fear and lack. These are part of your shadow self, and you must integrate and acknowledge them to let them go.

Make a decision to let go of your fears. Say the following statement aloud: "I allow my fears to dissolve. Everything that was holding me back is an illusion; I get that now. And I choose to step forward, fearless, into pure love. I will prioritize joy in my daily life. I infuse my body with love and joy. I let anything that is not for my highest good simply dissolve in a flood of gentleness, right now. I let go. I will let life and the heart of love lead me into pure bliss."

How do you feel after you say this aloud? Do you feel fizzing around you as your fears dematerialize? Do you feel relaxed? Do you feel anxious that things are going to change?

Change is good. In fact, it's one of the best things in the world. So embrace it. Constant change is the reality of existence. Why not enjoy it?

What are five things that would really make you feel good right now? Write down the list and go do one.

Let your fear dissolve and allow love to effervesce
through your being. Be open to feeling good in this moment.
#joyfulliving101

56. time for celebration

*Affirmation: "I celebrate who I am, what I love,
and all of my blessings that lead to joy."*

Your assignment today is to choose one or more things to celebrate. You can choose anything you'd like. There is an endless number of things to celebrate in your life in any moment. Celebration affirms the goodness and positive excitement in your life. And when you focus on and affirm something, you make life decisions that bring more of it into your life. Like attracts like, and what gets attention multiplies.

A celebration validates your life, and you are valid. You matter and deserve to be celebrated. So, think of something you can celebrate today. What amazing choices have you made lately? When have you shared your bounty or loved yourself? Pat yourself on the back. Affirm your validity in the world. You are celebration worthy!

Exercise: How to Celebrate

Bliss comes from daily celebrating. Some celebrations can be blowouts, and some can be quiet celebrations just for you. There are infinite ways to celebrate. Choose one or more from the list below or make up you own. Celebrate something today. It doesn't have to be a big deal to anyone but you. Maybe you stood up to someone without getting upset. Perhaps you found the perfect gift for your spouse or got all of your weekend cleaning done early and have a wide-open Sunday. Did you make it to the gym before work? Small things are just as celebration worthy as holidays.

Make a sign to adorn your celebration. It could say, "Happy Tenth Day of My New Job!" Or maybe, "Celebrate My Intelligence Day!" or, "Merry New Windshield Wipers Day!" Pick a celebration theme song and make it über upbeat. Play it, dance around, sing along, and change the words to fit your celebration. Get a group of friends together and go bowling or do some other activity to celebrate the weekend.

Want to get really silly? Have a tea party with some stuffed animals and your kids or nieces or nephews! You really celebrate when you get out of your normal routine and relax back into your innate childlike nature. Some of the most memorable moments are born of the slightly silly and outrageous.

To celebrate, you must step into your innate jovial nature. Get out. Have fun. Honor your life. Connect with the fun, jubilant, inner child who loves to celebrate. Feel her or him within you, completely ready to jump for you about life. You need more parties in your life. We all do! Commemorate the good and the great. Celebrate the ordinary and the extraordinary. Find the miraculous in each day. There is always *something* to celebrate, even if it's simply a cleansing rain. Appreciate that rain by splashing in puddles and enjoying the sensation of the rain running down your body. Then enjoy a bath at home to warm up.

Make life a celebration. Get yourself a special journal to record one thing to celebrate each day. Appreciate what you have, and you will attract more goodness. You will make choices that bring more goodness to you by celebrating all of your blessings. Your inner child will finally feel fulfilled to be himself or herself, someone who is meant to enjoy and to be in joy. You deserve a life worth celebrating. Go get it and appreciate it.

Each day offers a reason to celebrate.
Find it and experience true bliss.
#joyfulliving101

57. your true state

Affirmation: "*I am a limitless being of oneness.*
I am the physical embodiment of joy.
Anything is possible in my life. My true source is joy."

Your true state is limitless. You are a soaring spirit of pure joy. That is what you really are. Can you feel it deep within? Does the boundlessness of yourself beckon you? Do you dream of flying, skimming eternity with utter joy? Your spirit is unlimited. World traditions call this true state different names. In Sanskrit the word is *anahata*, which actually means "bliss."

A free, never-ending, joyful, multihued human is what you truly are. Embrace your true state. Feel how limitless you are.

Stand. Raise your arms straight up above your head. Stretch your body. Reach for the sky. Elongate your torso, arms, and legs. Reach and stretch.

You can be anything. You can do anything. Anything is possible. Stretch and feel this truth. Be limitless for this moment, with no inner naysayer or mind chatter to bring you down. Just be your boundless self for a few moments. Give yourself that gift. Your boundless self is your spirit, and you embody the endlessness of your spirit in your finite body.

Exercise: Stretch Your Limits

This exercise brings the energy of limitless possibility into your physical and mental bodies. When you stretch and physically engage your body, your brain is able to reach outside its usual comfort zone and think of new possibilities. What really happens is that you step into the universal flow. A new and ever-changing energy field becomes available to you. This is a place where your thoughts and willingness to participate in life are all you need to create the life of your dreams. You are your true source of joy and meaning.

Reach for the sky again. Stretch as high as you can. Reach and allow your mind to lighten and expand. Notice that its hold will loosen, and enter into limitless consciousness. Focus your attention on your brow center. This is the center of integration in many yogic traditions, and you are learning to integrate your boundless spirit with your human life and body. Repeat the word "joy." You might feel a pulse sensation in your brow center. As you physically and energetically stretch higher, you may feel lighter. While in this position of stretching, ask yourself, if all possibilities exist limitlessly, what would you create or change in your life? Brainstorm ten or more answers. Try to keep the feeling of stretching, but bring your arms down and grab your journal. Write your ideas down.

Now get to it! Start enacting your list. Make a plan by writing a date and estimated time next to each item for when you will do each one. Post it somewhere or keep it in your purse. Put the actions in your schedule.

In reality, everyone is unlimited. All limits are simply illusions. Understanding is the breeze that sweeps them away.
#joyfulliving101

58. HONORING YOUR HEART CONNECTIONS

Affirmation: "*I celebrate the connections in my life,*
from my past, present, and future.
I joyfully accept love in all of its healthy forms!"

Connecting to others is the main way you open your heart to the healing power of love. Love can refresh a tired spirit. It can repair your deepest wounds. It can give life a deeper meaning. Love is one of the riches of life. And it propels you to grow as a person and soul. And love enriches your spirit. The love you shared in this life is your celebration of human being-ness. It's beautiful.

Take some time to ponder love in your life. Feel how rich you are in love. This love wealth starts with yourself. Your self-love is something to be celebrated. How connected do you feel to yourself?

Self-connection and awareness are immense assets. Knowing yourself deeply helps you create the life you want because you know what you want. That is rarer than you'd think. What if you don't know what you want?

Exercise: What Do I Want?

Ask yourself the following questions and jot down the answers. See what comes up. Just write whatever comes to mind.

+ Who am I, really?
+ What do I want in life?
+ Who and what are my great loves in this life?
+ What do I want more of in my life?
+ How can I make that a priority?

Contemplate your answers. Knowing yourself in this way helps you connect to your true self.

Exercise: Throw a Connection Party

In this activity you are making a list. Bring your attention to your heart chakra in the center of your chest. Feel your heart chakra pulse with energy. Your consciousness is connecting to your heart center. Take a moment to feel beautifully connected to yourself.

Ask yourself, "Besides myself, who do I feel most connected to? Is this a healthy connection for my highest good?" If the answer is yes, write down that person's name.

Now, ask yourself, "Besides myself and the person I was just asking about, who do I feel most connected to? Is this a healthy connection for my highest good?" If the answer is yes, write down that person's name. Repeat that process so you list the top five people you feel most connected to.

Now plan a celebration! If you are all scattered around the world or have a tough time getting together, you can connect with each of these people individually on the phone or Skype. Share a few words of appreciation about what each person has brought to your life. This might sound like, "Jill, you have been a friend through ups and downs for almost twenty years. I want to celebrate how awesome you are. You are the most talented person I've ever met! Cheers!"

Whatever you say just needs to come from the heart. That's all. Share your gratitude and celebrate the connections in your life. And receive the love that flows back. Celebrate it!

The people we adore in our lives
brighten our days and illuminate our nights.
#joyfulliving101

59. working with animal messages

Affirmation: "*I love my animal allies and am grateful for their support. I accept it.*"

The natural world provides you with a rich tapestry of symbolism and energy from which to drink. Animals bring you messages all the time. These can be pets, wild animals, or spirit animals. You can be quenched by the vast love offered from your animal allies.

Have you ever felt like an animal you saw was delivering a message to you? It could have been a pet who knew you needed comfort after a tough day and lavished you with love, or it could be three hawks flying across your path in one day. Animals are messengers of universal life force. They are harbingers of the divine.

Synchronistic occurrences in your life are designed to awaken you to the world beyond the physical, mundane, day-to-day world you see before your eyes. Just beyond the veil an intricate, rich, magical world exists, consisting of currents of energy and sparkles of nature spirits. The world is vibrantly alive in the visible and invisible sense. Opening your spirit eyes to nonphysical reality can illuminate your life into Technicolor. It can enhance your bliss with meaning and interconnection.

In this chapter we will focus on animal allies to guide you into the reality just beyond the one you see before you with your physical eyes. Animals tap into the archetypal and instinctive within us. This opens our cellular memory to a time when connection with the primal nonphysical world was a way of life. This basic connection to our true nature is life affirming.

Exercise: Meet Your Animal Allies

Go outside to do this activity if possible. If you aren't able to, it will also work indoors.

Lie down or recline in a relaxed, seated position. Quiet your mind for a few minutes and get centered.

Say this invocation aloud: "I ask that all that transpires in this mediation be for the highest good of all life and in accordance with universal natural law. I now connect with the animal ally in my spirit family who is best suited to connect with me today. I welcome you in love and accept your love and goodness. Come sit next to me on my right, and let's connect."

Sit back and send your senses into the area around you. Your animal ally is going to come sit right next to you. Put out your hand to feel the animal. Do you sense what type it is? Have you ever met this being before in physical or nonphysical reality?

Greet it. Connect with your animal ally. Ask it if it has any messages for you. Listen. Converse. Spend time together. Ask your animal ally to send you three real-world signs in the next seven days. If you still aren't sure who the animal is, the signs may be about that, or they may be a message about your life or one telling you that you are not alone.

When you are done hanging with your animal ally, you can both say farewell and thank you. Sense the animal receding into the background of your awareness. It will go back to the periphery of your spirit family but will be near if you call it to connect again.

Animal allies are all around, offering beauty and connection.
#joyfulliving101

60. PRISMATIC COLOR

*Affirmation: "I jump into color bliss,
today and every day!"*

Some people really smell or hear color. They have synesthesia, a phenomenon in which two sensory pathways are simultaneously stimulated. Those people are often highly creative and intuitive.

Your vision is a sense for which to be supremely grateful. So much richness and beauty can be experienced through your eyes. The beauty of color can be seen in all its gloriousness. But what about your other senses?

Picture the color turquoise. What might it *sound* like?

Envision the color purple. What might it *smell* like?

How about vibrant fuchsia? What do you imagine it would *taste* like?

Beautiful bliss is offered up as a daily experience to us by the world of color. Start opening your senses to it and appreciating the abundance of beauty around you.

You can tap into your creative and intuitive gifts by consciously combining sensory sensations. For example, when you eat an orange, look at the color and enjoy the taste, smell, and feel of the juice. Then ask yourself what this color would *sound* like. If it was music, imagine it.

Think and feel out of the box with color to expand your cognitive function, create a richer life experience, and appreciate beauty. Find the bliss of color. It's all around!

Exercise: Colors of the Body

Playing with color can improve your mood and uplift your spirit, both of which are beneficial to your overall health. In this exercise you'll be doing just that in several different ways.

Gather some paper and colorful art supplies. Outline the silhouette of a person or draw a stick figure. Draw circles or spirals where each of the traditional seven chakras or energy centers is thought to exist: the tailbone or base of the spine, the navel, the solar plexus, the sternum, the throat, the center of the forehead, the top of the head.

Apply creative colors to the chakra illustration. Use any medium—colored glue, sand, foods, paints, etc. Do this intuitively; unfocus your eyes and let your rational mind disengage. The colors might not be in traditional "chakra order." Hang your drawing up and appreciate its beauty.

The more you work with color and light, the better you feel physically, mentally, emotionally, and spiritually. Enjoy colorful foods, put glasses of colored water on sunlit windowsills, create art using color, dance while connecting with different colors, try colored light bulbs in your home, and explore music and color at the same time.

You can say the following affirmative statement to increase your health with color: "I, _____ (your name here), am a Technicolor being. I am made of light and color. I exist in a world of supportive vibrancy, and my life is aligned with my infinite spectrum of color-being and light-being. Color vibration is my ally while enhancing my life with joy and perfection."

Vivid living is your destiny! You are a being of color and light.
Unleash your bliss.
#joyfulliving101

61. nature's support

Affirmation: "I am nature, and I am grateful."

Nature is a self-regulating system of balance, and humans are part of nature. *You* are part of nature, even if you are the most die-hard city person. You are nature. And nature has its own innate consciousness and intelligence.

Nature's consciousness wants to support you. The more you are part of nature, the more connected you feel and the more support you can accept from nature as a whole. You eat nature; it's your food. You drink nature; it quenches your thirst. You appreciate nature; it offers beauty. It's time to thank nature for your abundance.

What are all the many ways nature heals you? How does nature support you? How do you support nature?

When you walk outside, nature embraces you. It offers you gorgeous vistas for your eyes. It sings you sweet odes with song-birds and crickets. It offers you beautiful aromas from plants and flowers. Nature caresses your skin with gentle, pleasant breezes. And it gives you flashes of flavor that tantalize your taste buds from the foods you eat.

Nature mirrors you because you are nature. Yes, sometimes nature is a gorgeous, glistening sea brimming with tranquility and reflecting sunlight. But other times that sea roils under the powerful presence of a thunderstorm or hurricane. Sometimes, it is dramatically sucked up into a quick and potent waterspout. Everything exists in nature: creation, maturation, sharing, destruction, and rebirth. Nature teaches you about life.

Like nature, you create things, and sometimes through nature you create people. Like nature, you mature in different ways over time, and so do your ideas. Like nature, you share your bounty. Like nature, you destroy when you eat a living plant or drive over a living thing. And like nature, you are reborn through your learning and growth. But no matter what, life marches on, just like it does with nature. And one day when you transition out of your current body, your soul will move on to the next facet of nature it chooses to explore.

Nature offers bliss. It's in the pleasurable moments. The smell and sights of vibrant flowers, the sensory moments of swimming in clear waters, the gentle breezes, the exhilaration of dramatic lightning—you receive so much from nature with no thought of reciprocation. Nature gives freely so we can live and be happy. It's time to give back.

Exercise: Thanking Nature

In this exercise you will offer your gratitude to nature in order to become even more balanced as a part of nature. You are nature, and by thanking nature you can align with the world around you to experience more health and well-being and live more blissfully.

Gather some materials of your choice. Use natural materials from outside, like flowers, sticks, rocks, sand, seaweed, feathers, grass, soil, leaves, and bark. Choose to receive what is freely given, meaning choose a leaf that has already fallen as opposed to plucking one off a living tree.

Put your materials together and make something. You might use some glue or string. Create a beautiful nature sculpture.

Bring it outside, present it to nature, and speak aloud your heartfelt thanks. Sit there afterward and listen. Feel nature respond. Notice the elementals of the area too. They will love the sculpture. When you are done, say thank you and go about your day.

You are part of nature, and its pulse beats in your veins.
#joyfulliving101

62. creating a blissfully happy day

Affirmation: "*I am worthy of daily joy, and I will treat myself to a glorious day of complete bliss at least once per month.*"

You deserve a blissful, happy day. And you deserve that day to be every day! Create your best life with your consciously chosen actions, words, and thoughts. Find your bliss with decisive confidence.

This entry is all about what would make a truly blissful, truly happy, complete day for you. You need to give yourself a treat often. So we are going to lay it all out, and you are going to make it happen. Let's start by thinking about what bliss is to you.

- *Bliss:* What does that word evoke for you? What experiences create that feeling for you? Make a list.
- *Joy:* When you hear that word what do you picture? When do you feel true joy? Make another list.
- *Happiness:* In what moments have you felt perfectly happy? Do any peak experiences come to mind? List them.

Really listen to yourself and ponder what happiness is to you. Focus on your heart and what it feels like there when you experience bliss, joy, and happiness. Internalize the fact that you deserve to feel those feelings as much as humanly possible. You deserve to be happy. You deserve to be joyful. You deserve to be in total bliss because you are perfect exactly as you are. You matter, and this world needs you happy, healthy, and joyful. So let's find your blissful day today.

Exercise: Schedule a Day of Bliss

In this exercise you're going to use the lists that you've just made to plan a day of bliss just for yourself. It may seem strange to do this, because often we are so focused on making others happy that we forget about ourselves. Planning a day just for you will help remind you that you are important too.

Get out your calendar and your journal.

Look at the list that you just made about what bliss, joy, and happiness feel like for you. Now look at your calendar and find a day within the next thirty days that you can set aside one hundred percent for yourself. No work, no obligations, no kids (if you have them), no family—this is a day just for you. Pencil in that day of bliss.

Now let's plan it. Look at your list of blissful feelings and experiences from earlier. Which of those could you make happen that day? What could you do to evoke that feeling?

Would you feel blissful at the spa with your best friends? Or at the pool splashing in the sun?

Select something from the bliss category and put that into the schedule for that day.

Do the same thing from the joy and happiness categories. See if you can fit three really blissful, joyful, happy things into this day. You can do this by yourself or invite friends or family who only enhance you; no one who you have to take care of, babysit, counsel, or do anything but have complete unabashed fun with is allowed here.

As you plan this special day to celebrate your bliss, ask yourself how much laughter each possible activity will provide. How much joy and enjoyment will you experience? Indulge your senses on this day. Ignite your *joie de vivre*. Step outside your usual box and go for the peak experiences. You deserve it!

Make a commitment to schedule a day like this for yourself every month or so, and make joy and happiness a top priority, no matter what.

Set aside even one day just for fun,
and you will improve the next seven.
#joyfulliving101

63. SPIRITUAL DANCE

Affirmation: "I boogie my bliss, dance away my density, and jump into joy!"

Dancing has been part of the human experience since before recorded history. People have danced in groups and solitarily for millennia. Combining movement and music invokes something deep and instinctive within. It ignites internal rhythms, opens the doors for harmony and melody, and enlivens the brain.

Stomping your feet and clapping your hands creates sound and rhythm. These beats drive you forward and make you want to move. There's something instinctive within you that is driven to dance. It is the creative spirit within you, and it was one of the first creative impulses to awaken in the human race. Dancing releases feel-good chemicals that result in bliss.

Dance can be spiritual. It can be intentional. You've heard of tribes doing rain dances to inspire water for their crops? All through history, people have used dance for different intentions, like asking for favorable outcomes in their lives or urging the weather to go the way they would like.

You can use dance as a way to enhance your bliss, enact intentions, and put them out into the greater reality. Movement and music are powerful catalysts to move energy. And when you take an intention or desire and communicate it in a way that makes sound and movement, you increase the likelihood of it coming to pass.

You can harness the power of spiritual dance today!

Exercise: Bliss Boogie

In this exercise you're going to create your very own dance. The purpose of it is to experience bliss and to focus your thoughts into intentions or goals for yourself.

Create an intention for the dance you're about to do. It can be something simple, like feeling blissful, or it can be something more specific, like getting a new job as a museum docent.

Think about the feeling that your intention would create. And then, based upon that feeling, select a piece of music to be the soundtrack to your dance.

Put it on and begin to move. Think about the intention and feel the feeling as you dance.

Say or chant your intention as you dance. You can clap your hands, stomp your feet, snap your fingers, sing along, yell, or scream. You can dance away your density while you boogie your bliss. Let your dance happen organically, and go wherever it takes you. (You might need to dance away a fear in order to be aligned to get your museum docent job. Dance can do that!)

When the song finishes, you can repeat it and do more dancing, or you can select another song and keep the party going.

Spirituality and joy are not mutually exclusive. In fact, they are both enhanced by the other. You can get wild and crazy and dance your intention. Enjoy the dance of bliss that you have created.

Dance away your density and celebrate your splendor.
#joyfulliving101

64. treating yourself

Affirmation: "My heart is a blooming rose of self-love."

Treating yourself is a wonderful way to express your self-love. When you give yourself a gift or treat, even if it is small or has no monetary value, you are telling yourself that you are special. You communicate to yourself that you are worth celebrating.

It's powerful to show yourself on a regular basis how valuable you are. When you affirm your value by treating yourself and giving yourself moments and experiences that you know will feed your soul, you communicate how worthy you know you are. Each of these treats or gifts you give yourself builds your self-worth. They build self-esteem and help you discover your peak abilities. You have to believe in yourself and have confidence in yourself to dare to be different, to dare to be you.

Make a commitment to treat yourself like you would a treasured lover or a beloved child. Vow to give yourself validation and affirmation through your actions every day. That means taking the long way home from work to view your favorite sunset spot. It could mean going for a walk after lunch before returning to your daily activities. It could mean giving yourself a fashion magazine to read over the weekend. It could mean taking the time to go to the local health club and to swim and then relax in the sauna. Give yourself the message every single day that you are worthy of love. Then shower yourself with that love. Show yourself through your consciously chosen thoughts, words, and actions that you deeply value yourself.

What three treats could you give yourself this week? If you had a close friend you wanted to give a special gift, what would it be? If you wanted to give your significant other a romantic, relaxing experience, what would that be? If you wanted to give your delightful child or niece or nephew something to make them feel special, what would that be? Consider giving these gifts to yourself. And they need not be physical things; they might be activities or experiences or anything you choose.

Exercise: Love Roses for a Lovely Person

This week, challenge yourself to pick out the most beautiful, dazzling bunch of roses you can find. Pick your absolute favorite color roses. This is not about spending money: they could be ones you have grown, or maybe you just buy a single perfect rose instead of a dozen. You could even make your roses out of construction paper, or paint them with paints on a canvas. The point is to give yourself roses that represent love. These roses are from you and to you. They are symbolic of how much you love yourself. You are worth it! Watch your bliss expand as you can feel your love and value affirmed from within. This is your inner power. Tap into it and experience pure bliss.

Imagine a brilliant rose of pure love in your heart.
Next, see a twinkling flower within the hearts of all you meet.
#joyfulliving101

65. GUIDING LIGHTS

Affirmation: "*My ancestors offer me bliss, love, and light.*
I gratefully receive that which is for my highest good and release
the rest back into the pure, white light."

You have so many ancestors, and they are all eternal in the space of love. You may know about some of them, and there may be many that you have never heard of before. You have an endless, benevolent crowd of ancestors positively cheering you on from all over the universe. When spirits leave their bodies, all kinds of unique things happen, but eventually they end up back in communion with the universal heart of love. And from that space, they often shine a unique and benevolent light on those who hailed from their lineage after they left the earth.

You may have many ancestral spirits that you met before they passed away or heard of from family members. It's likely you also have many other ancestral spirits available that you've never heard of. There are endless positive, loving members of your extended family smiling down on you.

This truth speaks of the eternal nature of bliss. Souls can find bliss both when incarnated and when in nonphysical reality. You can attract your blissful, benevolent, high-vibrational ancestors and invite them to help you and ease your journey in this life.

Oftentimes it is a great learning experience for the ancestral spirits to be around you. Cheering you on and helping you out gives them a unique and special job. Everybody wins!

Think about the things different family members have said to you on this topic over the years. For example, maybe your mother says that she sometimes senses her grandfather with her, your grandmother knows that her favorite uncle is around the house in a certain room, or somebody on your father's side knows that there are generations of people before him who help the family.

It's likely that many ancestral spirits want to pay it forward. They want to share their caring and goodness with you now that they have returned to the heart of love. Let them enhance your bliss!

Exercise: Ancestral Allies

Get a piece of paper and pen and write the following statement: "I invite my highest-vibrational, loving, benevolent ancestral spirits to bless me with their love and support as needed for my highest good and the highest good of all life. You may visit me very gently in my dreams with only loving, joyful, blissful, and positive messages. These interactions will only enhance us both and leave me feeling completely rested and rejuvenated in the morning. I ask that I easily remember these interactions and that the entire experience is always for my highest good."

Take the piece of paper, fold it up, and place it in your pillowcase tonight. You can leave it there as long as you want. Keep a journal next to your bed so that when you wake up in the morning, you can quickly write down any fragments of memory from your loving ancestral interactions.

Ancestors from all times have shared their essence with you.
Accept the light and let go of the rest.
#joyfulliving101

66. Respect Yourself

Affirmation: "*I respect myself and receive joy from all directions.*"

Feeling amazing creates great joy. Enjoying life, experiencing pleasure, and feeling great are necessary ingredients to living your bliss. You deserve to feel amazing. You deserve to treat yourself. You deserve to enjoy your life, your senses, your relationships, and the love in your heart. You deserve ultimate bliss. Go after it! Feel amazing today!

You must respect yourself to feel amazing. You have to know that you are worth the effort of putting in the time and energy to create a life of bliss. You have to do everything in your power to drill that into your brain, no matter how stubborn you might be.

You are worthy of respect and kindness. You must respect yourself and respect your desire to live a life of bliss. You must take action to put that into practice every day. You are responsible for your life. Take ownership of it now.

Why would little old you be worthy of respect and kindness? Because you exist! Because you are a radiant soul of light. Because you are beautiful. No matter who you are, where you've been, what you've done, what your parents told you, or what society told you, you are extraordinary.

You are the only one who can take responsibility to create your extraordinary life.

Exercise: Trusting Yourself

Get out your journal. Write down this statement: "I am worthy of respect and kindness; I am sacred." "Sacred" means precious, special, and a treasure of true beauty. That's you!

Here is your real challenge. You must make a commitment, right now, to live this truth from this day forward. That means whatever you say about yourself will be only steeped in respect, kindness, and loving sacredness for yourself. Nothing else. You may never say an unkind word about yourself again. Make this commitment now. Write down what it means to you and what it might be like. Write down your commitment with decisive confidence. Make some powerful decrees about how you treat yourself right now.

Next, you must make a commitment to act in accordance with honoring your worthiness of respect and kindness and honoring your sacredness. Every action must reflect your love for yourself. No other options but loving yourself and acting that way are on the table anymore. Write down this truth and how you feel about it.

Endeavor only to think kindly and respectfully about yourself. If you catch yourself thinking, saying, or doing anything that is contrary to this tenant, gently stop, notice, and make a decision to change it right away. There's no judgment when you slip. To err is human; to forgive yourself is divine. And to be responsible for loving, respecting, and honoring yourself is the ultimate accomplishment in your life. Kudos!

Now you can trust yourself. You have no question about how respectfully you will insist upon being treated. Get ready to feel free! Get ready for soaring bliss! You are the source of your bliss, and you just stepped into it.

> *Love yourself like you would a treasured lover*
> *or a cherished child.*
> *#joyfulliving101*

67. try new experiences

Affirmation: "I embrace new experiences every day. I revel in the fun adventures I create for myself and absorb their blissful gifts."

Daily bliss is deeply enhanced by novelty. The interesting and stimulating in your life keep things vibrant and engaging. Getting stuck in a rut happens when we don't try new experiences. So instead of monotony, sometimes we must choose adventure. New horizons reveal that we have only scratched the surface of possibility and there are still exciting opportunities to learn and grow.

New adventures tell you, "There is more to uncover here." New experiences keep you engaged and loving life. They dangle the enticing carrot of discovery before you, saying, "Here is a new challenge" or "Don't miss the fun!"

Let yourself wake up to new dimensions by trying things you may not have tried before. You will find new ways of thinking and being. Newness increases your vitality. You have more sparkling, crackling aliveness to yourself. You also feel more creative and more apt to get up off your couch and create something. With each new positive experience, your bliss level will soar.

Reach out of your comfort zone and plan weekends of newness. Identify day trips to fun new places. Preparing for new experiences and adventures is part of the fun. The anticipation brings a burst of zest to your life. A richer, more colorful palette of experiences is available to you as you become open to newness. Pack a lunch and get going!

When you try something new, you are transported into a scene that you have never been in. How will you behave? What will be your favorite part? New experiences give us a chance to get to know ourselves better and discover new parts of ourselves. If you grab a friend, family member, or spouse to join you on a new adventure, you learn about them too. How do they respond to new moments? What do they love doing?

New experiences bring us into a more playful mindset. We find our inner child a bit. We let go more. We relax into life, yet we are engaged because of the newness. These two ingredients, novelty and play, are a recipe for stress relief. Yes! Seemingly elusive and much sought, relief from the daily grind and its stress is worth a bit of effort.

Exercise: Every Day Is New

Make a list of the top ten new things on the planet you would most like to experience. They can be large or small experiences, from visiting the pyramids to trying the newest coffee drink, but aim for half or more to be accessible on a daily basis.

Why are these experiences important to you? Make a vow to yourself that you will do at least one of those things daily for the next week. Which experience will you focus your attention on today? What step can you take now to move closer to making that happen?

Next, outline what step would follow the first step. Do you need to prepare anything or just do it? What are the rest of the steps to make that experience happen for you?

Commit now to taking these steps, following through in ways that will propel you to live new, novel, engaging experiences. Write the following statement in your journal: "I, _____ your name here), being of sound mind, body, and spirit, choose to restructure my priorities to accommodate enjoying and learning from life through new experiences. I allow these experiences to flow forth from my endless supply of potential experiences."

Begin to plan your next fresh experience soon after your first. Prioritizing novelty and excitement in your life keeps you engaged and joyful.

Fresh moments ignite the senses. Create them.
#joyfulliving101

68. coming to self-acceptance

Affirmation: "*I love myself totally, completely,
and unconditionally.*"

Deep inside you lies a treasure trove of goodness as well as a shadow side. It is time for you to know yourself, your true self. No more pretenses and false fronts. Just the real you. No filter. No shame or worry about who you really are. To know yourself is to know the divine. You are a sacred, beautiful being worthy of respect, kindness, love, and all good things. And all that goodness starts with the ultimate gift you can give yourself: self-acceptance.

Your shadow self is the part of you that stays hidden away for nobody to see. Occasionally, you might catch a glimpse of it in a moment of partially suppressed rage or stark loneliness. The shadow is a very personal aspect of the total self; everything you find unpalatable, unattractive, or socially unacceptable is a part of you, no matter how deeply it is buried within. Your shadow can be scary, for it contains all that you fear, especially about yourself—your inner malice, jealousy, envy, and madness. It's the sad, little child hiding in the corner after being rejected, and it's the bully on the playground who terrorizes others. It's the power-hungry monster within, and it's the helpless, supplicant victim. Your shadow is everything you can't control, your very own personal, inner chaos.

How can you dig deep and find true acceptance? How can you find your real self? Start by telling yourself, "Self, I am here to accept you. I have a no-questions-asked policy; if you share a deep secret, I will accept it. I will stand by you, self, because I love you."

Really tell yourself that and feel how powerful it is. Do you notice it resonating within you? If you do, it is because no one is completely perfect according to societal standards. Everyone has faults, secrets, and challenges along with talents, gifts, and qualities they flaunt. The thing is all of it is actually a treasure because it's you.

The more you integrate your deep self, the more you are free to accept and share joy and love. The energy of the parts that aren't accepted (like anger, fear, shame, rage, and jealously) can become clogged and stuck. They can affect your health and well-being, but love and acceptance are the balm that heals all wounds and clears all debts. They smooth your life and prepare you for greatness.

Exercise: Integrative Meditation

In this meditation we will work with facing our shadow side honestly so that we can come to a level of self-acceptance. Find a quiet space and lie down or sit comfortably. You will be going within, into your heart space. See yourself standing in a temple in the center of your heart. Notice the surroundings. What colors and textures do you see? Walk over to the altar in the center of the temple. If it is bare, cover it with things that bring you joy, like flowers, tropical fruits, minerals, pictures, artwork, or statues of deities. Stand and raise your arms above your head. See yourself doing the same within your heart's temple. Speak the following aloud with clarity of intention: "I call all aspects of my self to the center of my heart chamber. All are welcome in the temple; you will be received with love. My shadow, hear my call. It is time to integrate, shadow self, shadow self, shadow self." You are literally talking to your shadow self, and it helps if you say it aloud so that your brain and all of the parts of yourself physically hear you. If you speak your call aloud, you will have better results. See your shadow stand before you in the center of your heart temple. Do not judge it. Look it straight in the eye. Know it.

Visualize white light and love emanating from your spirit self, from your hands and heart and eyes, toward your shadow. When you feel a connection to your shadow self, ask it to speak to you. What does it have to say that you haven't been able or willing to hear? Listen without judgment.

Consider the possibility of opening your heart to loving your shadow. Try to allow that to happen now. Visualize opening your arms to hug your shadow.

If you are able to love yourself, you can integrate all aspects of who you are, whether or not they are consciously expressed. Then they won't express themselves unconsciously when you react to stressful situations or are triggered by circumstances. When people "blow up" in anger, it is their shadow part that is angry. When your shadow is done hugging you, offer it a home in your heart temple. Show it around and visualize helping it create a lovely room full of what will make it happy.

Sit for a time, noticing how you feel after welcoming all that you are into the temple of your heart. Do you notice anything new? A sense of wholeness or balance that wasn't felt before?

Use this process as often as you would like. Know that you have delved deep, found the beautiful depths of yourself, and freed yourself to accept and live more joy.

Accept yourself. Accept your flaws, quirks, talents, secret thoughts—all of it—and experience true liberation.
#joyfulliving101

69. ONE DAY ONLY

Affirmation: "*I embrace every day as an opportunity to live fully and with total heart!*"

What if you had one day left on earth? What would you do? Would you want to make sure everyone in your life who cared about you knew? Would you commune with spirit in deep meditation? Would you party like a wild child? Would you create the most glorious art or music?

One day only. What would you do?

Would you spend the day crying over losing your attachments? Or would you look forward to the next phase of your soul's adventure?

Many faced with this question think of those they love. We feel the attachment. The reality is that we are connected in love for all time. Love doesn't require physical proximity: it transcends space and time.

Today could be your one day. Do you have the courage to plant a big kiss on it? This isn't supposed to inspire fear or sadness but, conversely, joy. Be in bliss for a life well lived. Start living right and stop playing small. Be huge.

Exercise: One Day of Massive Love

With only today to live, many people would want to make sure that those they loved knew just how much they are adored. In order to live for today, we will embrace those we care for in this exercise. By doing this, we will deepen our connections and feel gratitude for our connections and the joy they bring. Who needs to be told that you love them? If this were your last day, who would you want to know you care?

Make a list. Try to tell them every day. Some ways to do that are with a greeting card, verbally, through an e-mail, by posting a picture of you together on Instagram, by sending them a gift, by offering them your time, by sharing your attention, and by giving a valentine.

Every day, tell your heartmates that you love them. All the love energy flowing from you will return in a cascade of love to you. Ride that wave home, and be in bliss.

Every day could be your last, so share your love far and wide
with everyone you adore.
#joyfulliving101

70. Connecting with Nature

Affirmation: "*I am one with all life.*
I am connected to all the goodness in all the universes."

Nature can inspire feelings of transcendence and spiritual connection. You can feel the energy in nature. When you take a walk on the beach, your cares melt away. When you hike an old growth forest, your problems seem insignificant, and you relax. Sometimes we aren't on a pristine beach or in a majestic forest, but we can still connect with nature wherever we are. The following exercise will help you build that connection.

Exercise: Interconnection Is All Around

If you can get outside, perfect. If not, position yourself so you can see out a window. Get settled and comfy. Observe your natural surroundings. Notice their energy and presence. Appreciate their beauty.

If it is daytime, check out the clouds. If you are gazing at a totally cloudless sky, notice the birds or stones around you. If it is night, look at the stars, or if it's cloudy, observe the trees or plants nearby.

Settle on one thing to pay attention to, such as clouds or stars. Start to expand your perspective as if your peripheral vision is widening. Keep your eyes facing the center and count how many of the clouds or stars you can see in one snapshot of your vision. Is it a lot? Notice their beauty.

Now look around, turning your head to see as much as you can from your perch. How many of your clouds or stars do you count? Is it many more than your single field-of-vision snapshot or a similar amount?

Sometimes noticing, and even quantifying, beauty can highlight it. Even if you are in a crowded city, there are still clouds and stars to remind you of the fact that you are surrounded by nature's beauty. This shows us grace in our environment no matter where we are.

Bring your attention to the fact that you are connected to each cloud, each star, each rock, each bird, each leaf, each plant—everything. All is connected. Each star is part of you. Each blade of grass out your window is connected to you because you are literally made of the same elements as everything that surrounds you, just in different quantities.

Slowing down and noticing your environment and the magnificence in nature wherever you are helps you feel the truth that you are one with all! Appreciate that amazing spiritual knowing today. It is a gift.

Nature offers splendor and artistry for us to appreciate.
Opening our senses reveals we are surrounded by magnificence.
#joyfulliving101

71. CHILD's eyes

Affirmation: "My life is wondrous, and I appreciate it every day!"

We often forget the wonder and awe with which we saw the world as children. Everything was exciting and new. Digging in the dirt was enthralling. Biking on a deserted street was an adventure. Trying a new kind of ice cream was a flavor-blasting treat. As you've gotten older, it's likely that some of the wonder of life has faded. Daily responsibilities and the pressures of life might have dulled your experiences. Your focus may be less on enjoyment and appreciation and more on survival and managing tasks. That is okay. It's natural and oh so common.

Sometimes bringing your attention to cultivating a sense of wonder can yield great dividends, like bliss, appreciating beauty, joy, and new zest for life. How might you be able to do that in your life? You could consciously choose to notice how amazing it is that your Zumba class of fifty people is completely dancing in unison. You could make a decision to appreciate the bald eagle you saw on the way to work. You could look with wonder into your own child's eyes and marvel at their existence.

Your everyday world is filled with miraculous experiences. You type on a machine and instantaneously send your words anywhere in the world. You breathe in air, and it is broken into useable pieces and sent all through your body to give you life. At any moment, you could endeavor to learn to speak an entirely new language. How wondrous!

Exercise: Wonder Writing

It's good to take a step back and look at the world from a new perspective. One way to do this is to write about your experiences in a way that's different from how you normally would.

Get your journal and start an entry called "Wonder Writing." List out the dates for the next week. Start with today. Think back on your day and view it with a child's eyes. What wondrous thing did you experience today? Write it down.

Each night this week, go back and repeat this exercise. Then at the end of the week, read through and notice how amazing your life actually is. It's beautiful! Find the wonder!

Extraordinary wonder and joy are woven through ordinary life.
Hunt for them relentlessly.
#joyfulliving101

72. CYBER GRATITUDE

Affirmation: "*I am grateful in life and online.*
My gratitude raises my vibration and enhances my joy."

Many of us spend an amazingly large part of every day online. Here in the Western world, our smartphones, tablets, and computers are at our side most of the day. We interact with friends, family, acquaintances, and colleagues online all day and into the night. We make connections online. Some of these connections are people who turn out to be friends. Some of them turn out to be bad dates. Some turn out to be business collaborators. We can show our personal traits online just like we would in the real world. If somebody is friendly in real life, it is likely that they will be friendly online. If somebody is more of an observer in real life, then they may observe online too. The anonymity of the Internet gives us a filter through which we can interact with the global society.

The questions for not only your online life but also your real-world life are these: How would you like to behave? What impact would you like to make on your world? What would you like to be a force for in the lives of the people with whom you come into contact? I suspect the answers are goodness, love, kindness, and happiness for many who are reading this book. Most people desire to be good people. Most people want to help others. Most people have good hearts. And how we behave online is an extension of that.

Expressing gratitude, caring, and interest in the people you meet online shows them that you believe that they matter. This extends your reach and the reach of your love all over the planet! In a way like never before in history, we have an opportunity to share our caring with people on the other side of the world.

Like many of you, I spend time online, and that includes being active on social media. When people like what I have to say, they quote me or repost my words. I love when people are encouraged by something I wrote, so I think it is wonderful when my followers share what I've said to their own friends. Because of that, I try to thank everyone who shares or quotes me. Some days I just can't get to everyone, but gratitude is always my priority.

The results of the cyber gratitude are amazing! People outpour their gratitude back! Everyone is so happy to be thanked. People are honored that somebody cares. I have even made friends this way, due to conversations that have sprung up afterward, and not to mention numerous wonderful, helpful business contacts.

Kindness, politeness, and giving thanks ingratiate you to others, but they also help you spread your love and caring. And the more you share of yourself, the happier you feel. Cyber gratitude will help enhance your bliss. You will feel joyful and happy for sharing and caring in your global community.

The friendships I have made include people in the Maldives, the Philippines, Singapore, Spain, Brazil, France, South Africa, and Peru. These people all resonate with the message of caring and kindness, and they participate in life! The Internet and globalization of our society have given us an opportunity to spread our gratitude worldwide in every direction to all people we encounter. Take this opportunity and run with it!

Exercise: Cyber Gratitude Bonanza

Now is a perfect time to express your gratitude to your online connections. Go on several of your social media profiles. Take a look at the people who like and comment on the things you post.

Notice who retweets or responds to the things that you had to say. Set aside twenty minutes right now and thank every one of them. And even beyond that, compliment them. Look at their profile, notice the goodness that they are putting out in the world, and affirm it.

You can be a force of good while sitting in your house on any device. Sadly, the Internet has its share of bullies and "trolls," people who seem to be online simply to make others feel small. By spreading positivity you can help drown out those negative

voices and spread more love. Immerse yourself in gratitude and
feel the bliss of sharing and caring, online and in real life.

You never know whose tough day you will brighten
with a few kind words. Tweet your positivity today!
#joyfulliving101

73. peace and calm

Affirmation: "Joyful peace pervades my being for all time."

Happiness in your heart creates contentment, peace, and calm that can enhance your life. Joy and happiness make your life feel full, rich, and complete. With a life like that and a happy heart, you can find true peace within.

Even if your joyful experiences are amped up and exciting, they will actually provide the perfect counterpoint to let you experience the pleasure of calmness and the easiness of peace. You will feel the joy of relaxation. Everyone needs downtime and a chance to revive and restore. Everyone needs tranquility and serenity; everyone needs peace and calm. Your joy enables you to have this in a healthy, happy way.

We all need rest amid the ebb and flow of life. Balance helps you maintain health and a positive outlook. Sometimes there are euphoric highs and joyful celebrations, and sometimes you spend quiet days at home curled up with a flavorful cup of tea and a warm blanket. Those types of moments provide us comfort and ease, and we need that along with all the euphoric joy we can stand. Give yourself the gift of a calm and quiet mind. Give yourself a gift of peace, calm, and all that is tranquil.

Exercise: Relax into Bliss

This activity will open you to the calm side of bliss. It'll help you sink into peacefulness so that you can feel happiness more deeply in your heart.

Lie down and close your eyes. Focus on your breathing, and let yourself begin to uncoil and unwind. Let the stress of the week slip away for a few minutes. Really feel the couch or bed beneath you, how it's supporting you, and how it's providing a foundation for you to find rest and ease. Feel grateful for that.

Now, bring your attention to the palms of your hands. Notice if they're buzzing or relaxed, if they feel lifeless or full of life. Bring your attention to your brow center, the point right between your eyebrows. Keep your attention there as you feel the pulse and energy of that area. Keep bringing your attention back there. Feel that brow center.

Now bring your attention to the arches of your feet. Feel that pulse. Bring your attention to your knees and feel that pulse. Do the same with your hips, your navel, the center of your chest, and the center of your throat.

Bring your attention back to the brow center. Let peace and calm wash over you, and let your mind rest. Keep your energy there to restore your vitality and charge back up. Experience the bliss of relaxation amid an energized body and quiet mind.

When you are ready, say aloud, "I am blissfully at peace, and I carry this through the rest of my day." Return to daily life.

You can use this quick activity to give your inner battery a recharge. You can recharge your body, mind, and heart with this quick experience of peace and calm.

Cultivating daily calm, even for a few minutes,
yields a core of centered wellness.
#joyfulliving101

74. move your body

Affirmation: "Moving my body ignites my bliss.
I say yes to movement!"

Moving your body can be very creative, whether it's through dancing, interpretive movement, mime, or sports. Movement is creative. When you move, you are physically expressing what is within you. And its exciting! If it's dance, it may be something especially artistic. If it's interpretive movement, then you may be expressing your imagination. If it's mime, you may be expressing the theatrical side within you. If it is sports, then you may be expressing your capacity and desire to achieve. All of these integrations of your creativity into physical expression pay large and health-enhancing dividends.

Moving your body is intrinsically healthy. It brings more vitality into your energy system. It ignites wildness in you. It revs up your hormonal and chemical systems and releases endorphins and feel-good chemicals. It helps you strive to translate what is within you to the external world using your physical body. Movement is so very healthy.

Exercise can ignite your creativity. By giving you those feel-good chemicals, it allows you to really tap into biological bliss.

You're getting blissed out on exercise. That's why it's so important to make exercise, movement, and fun part of your daily routine. At least several times a week, dance, play, jump, swim, shake your groove thing, play baseball, roller-skate, or just move your body. Do whatever moves you.

You have the power to increase your health and quality of life through movement. Movement brings your body and soul into balance. Movement makes you healthy, happy, and sparkling. Movement ignites your drive for the unlimited. Movement gives you confidence. Movement heals.

Exercise: Get Your Booty Blissful

This chapter serves as a call to action. It asks you to make a commitment to pleasant, fun-enhancing movement on a daily basis. Below is a list of some things you can do. Give them a try. You can create your own schedule of daily fun movement. Dance, stomp, or run straight into joy, and don't look back!

- Sway to music.
- Take a Latin dance class.
- Vacuum the house while dancing with music blasting.
- Practice soccer.
- Play Frisbee in the park.
- Do yoga.
- Run a race.
- Swing on a playground swing.

- Try a 5Rhythms class, a form of dance movement based on patterns and waves pioneered by Gabrielle Roth.
- Go for a walk.
- Use the stairs at work while repeating a happy mantra, like the word "joy," with each step.
- Plant some flowers, which involves digging and moving.
- Comb a beach for shells.
- Hike a trail.
- Try playing softball.
- Enjoy water aerobics.
- Dig a fire pit.
- Sample a Continuum Movement class, a type of movement created by the late Emilie Conrad and based on the joyful fluidity of the body.
- Lift weights.
- Decorate your yard with strings of lights and enjoy the stretching and fresh air.
- Explore Nia movement and dance, which combines dance, martial arts and healing arts.
- Dive deep into a pool, lake, or sea.
- Roll down a hill.
- Play hide and seek.
- Go roller-skating with friends.

- Get a Thai massage, which includes lots of stretching and movement.
- Sample different kinds of martial arts.

Moving your body moves energy. You can create or demolish whatever you need with kinetic dynamism.
#joyfulliving101

75. bath of bliss

Affirmation: "*My inner waters are healthy, balanced, and full of bliss for all time.*"

Taking a bath is a powerful symbol of relaxation. You are shown often in books, movies, and television how a relaxing bath can wash away the stress of the day and soothe the soul. This is true! Baths are really relaxing. Being immersed in water brings you to a primordial place, perhaps because you began in the water.

When you float in the tub, you give yourself an opportunity to let yourself unwind. You give the cerebrospinal fluid, a clear fluid found in the brain and spine, in your body a chance to rest and repattern. You give yourself an invitation to renew. Bath time is deeply healing and dramatically increases your quality of life. Give yourself the gift of a bath frequently. Let the act of taking a bath be a testament to your love for yourself. The fact that you take the time to soothe your soul in a warm and inviting bath demonstrates that you love yourself. It shows your inner being that it is valued, honored, and appreciated.

Imagine that your bathwater is made of bliss. Immerse yourself in bliss today!

Exercise: Bliss Bath Time

This exercise is all about pampering yourself and giving yourself a chance to relax and recharge, while bringing your inner and outer selves into balance and harmony.

Draw yourself a nice warm bath. Slip into the bath and use a towel or bath pillow to support your neck and head. You might choose to add sea salt, Epsom salt, bath clay, or essential oils to your bath.

As you lay in the bath close your eyes and relax yourself. Focus on the word "bliss." Repeat it while you bring your attention to your brow center, the spot between your eyebrows.

Feel the word bliss reverberate through your body. Let the word bliss charge the water in which you are laying. Bliss is a very high vibrational energy, and it feels good. Let your body and the water be filled with the essence of bliss

Now, invite your body's inner fluids to come into optimum balance. Say aloud, "I allow the fluids in my body to gently move into optimum, healthy, highly vibrational balance. This happens right now with no effort on my part, and this balance remains for all time. My body is joyful. My heart is full of bliss. And I rest in deep balance and ultimate harmony."

Hang out and enjoy your bath. Soak up the bliss because you love yourself and are worth it.

Sometimes a self-love soak can right the world
and recharge the heart. Draw a bath and step into bliss.
#joyfulliving101

76. Happy Helpers

*Affirmation: "I accept love and bliss from benevolent,
highly vibrational spirit friends for my highest good."*

In the infinite and eternal nature of existence, you will find that
there are infinite numbers of physical and nonphysical beings
who are focused on love and light. You can begin to meet some
of these beings and expand your perception of reality to encompass greater and greater truth.

The rule of thumb with these kinds of interactions is to keep
your focus on light, joy, happiness, and bliss. The other very important piece is to ask that everything that you do with these
beings and in these interactions be for the very highest good of
all life and in accordance with universal natural law, helping all
and harming none. Then you will have a very positive experience
befriending all kinds of interesting, benevolent beings.

There are so many friendly spirits waiting to meet you.
Some of the spirits have lived for trillions of years, so they've
been around the block. They are happy to share time, space, and
energy with you. They want to help; they understand, to different degrees, the challenge and gift of being human. They are
compassionate toward you. They want to help you reach your

goals and feel good while you are on this earth. After that, who knows what will happen? You might turn out to have hundreds of thousands of spirit friends. The possibilities are limitless. How blissful!

Exercise: Meet and Greet with a Bliss Goddess

A benevolent, loving bliss goddess would like to visit you today. What an auspicious day! It is a powerful and exciting experience to connect with a specific goddess about a specific thing, like bliss. It helps you feel like you are really getting to know nonphysical beings and helps you explore the expanded nature of reality, going deeper into the notion that not all life has a physical body. The goddess known as Tara is present with you now. Have you heard of her?

She is well known in Eastern mythology. Some people also believe that she has Celtic roots. The amazing thing about deities in mythology is that they, too, have experienced many different kinds of existences. So a goddess like Tara has experienced lives as a fairy or elemental, as many different kinds of animals and plants, as a monk, as a teacher, and as multitudinous others all over the universe.

She likes to focus on bliss now. She's a nonphysical being who helps people with many different types of things. She has come to you today to bring buckets and buckets of bliss. She offers you bouquets of bliss and showers you with blooms and bliss petals. Accept all these flowers and all this bliss!

Sit in a position where you can be comfortable and rested but still sitting up. Close your eyes for a minute and feel Tara in the room with you. She would never crowd you. She always respects your space. If you feel comfortable, stretch your two hands out and place them with your palms facing up in front of you. You can rest them on your knees if that is comfortable for you.

With your palms facing up, say aloud, "Tara, I invite you now to connect with me gently for the highest good of all life and in accordance with universal natural law, helping all and harming none."

Feel Tara sit before you. Just relax, keep your eyes closed, and be open as she hovers her palms over yours. You may sense her presence. You may feel pulsing, tingling, heat, or cold sensations in your hands. You may perceive color or flowers. You may hear music like a chime. You may feel a heart feeling. You may just know that she is there.

Sit that way together and let your palms exchange energy with her spirit palms. Notice what that feels like. When you're ready, you can introduce yourself. You can either do this aloud or with your mind. Tell her your name and thank her for coming to meet you.

Then listen with your heart as she introduces herself. Just be in a receptive space and take in whatever comes to you. Now ask her if she would like to share the feeling of pure bliss with you. She will eagerly respond yes!

If you'd like, relax as she uploads ultimate bliss through her being and into your hands. This upload is totally clean, totally clear, and made only of absolute pure bliss. Receive it, and when you feel the download is complete, thank her. You can stay and have a longer conversation with her or exchange more energy for as long as you'd like. You can ask for her to help you with your life or for anything you'd like.

When the experience is complete, feel yourself disconnect from her within the work you did. You can even say, "I now disconnect from Tara as needed for my highest good. Thank you so much, dear friend!"

And then you're done! You just made friends with a goddess. You can do this exercise again and again to connect with your new friend Tara.

Unleash the force of bliss within you.
Radiate your joy no matter what!
#joyfulliving101

77. JUMP FOR JOY

Affirmation: *"I jump for joy every day. My body pulses with joy, and my vibration soars. I feel amazing."*

Joy is your birthright. You were supposed to be born into a world of joyful ecstasy. It may have been a bumpy ride on the planet, but you can claim your joy now.

Joy is about movement and action. It's about jumping, stomping, laughing, dancing, flying, and swimming. Joy is an idea, but it's also an action or state of being. You can *do* joy. You also can *be* joy. You embody joy. Joy can pervade every part of your life if you let it.

Exercise: Joy Jumping

Go outside or find a brightly lit, colorful spot in your home. Plant your feet squarely on the ground and feel connected to the earth. If you are in your home or indoors somewhere, bring your awareness to the floor and think about the earth beneath it, even if it is one or more floors below.

Say aloud, "I choose joy in this moment, from a powerful, deep, strong core of radiance within me." Bend your knees and launch yourself into the air by jumping, and yell the word "joy." Do this three times in a row. Joy. Joy. Joy.

Feel your feet on the ground again and the earth beneath you. Feel the energy running through your body. It might feel hot or tingly.

Do your joy jumping again three more times in a row. Joy. Joy. Joy. Feel the energy running through your body. Feel your heart beating. Feel the world around you pulsing. How high did you jump? Can you jump higher?

Do one last round of three joy jumps. Joy. Joy. Joy.

Feel the energy of joy coursing through your body. This is the energy you need to feel every single day. This is the energy that will power your life to heights of success, pinnacles of performance, and a bonanza of bliss. Jump for joy today and every day.

The jump toward joy encompasses your life with boundless energy.
#joyfulliving101

78. animated adventures

*Affirmation: "I am animated by my joyful life.
I let my inner child feel loved and experience joy every day."*

What if it's a dreary and rainy day and you want your daily joy? What should you do? What if it is a snowy, chilly night and you want to laugh and feel enlivened and even childlike? Then you might need an animated adventure! Animation and cartoons take you back to a time when you were lighter and freer. You had less responsibility, fewer burdens, and more ease.

Those moments when you watched a fun cartoon as a kid allowed the world to slip away and your imagination to find delight. Why not give yourself that gift again? Pick out an animated movie and indulge your inner child. What were your favorite cartoons as a kid?

The list below is designed to give you some ideas of movies you might want to watch. It's separated into decades so you can find one that reminds you of happy times in your childhood.

+ 1960s: *The Sword in the Stone, The Jungle Book, 101 Dalmatians, The Incredible Mr. Limpet, Dr. Seuss' How the Grinch Stole Christmas!*

- 1970s: *The Aristocats, Robin Hood, Bedknobs and Broomsticks, Pete's Dragon, The Rescuers*
- 1980s: *The Fox and the Hound, The Little Mermaid, The Land Before Time, My Neighbor Totoro, The Great Mouse Detective*
- 1990s: *The Lion King, Toy Story, Aladdin, Mulan, A Bug's Life*
- 2000s: *Shrek, Kung Fu Panda, Finding Nemo, The Incredibles, Madagascar*
- 2010s: *How to Train Your Dragon, Despicable Me, Frozen, Tangled, Brave*

Exercise: I Am Animated

What if you were to create a little animated adventure of your own? It could be all about you! This is an activity for the child within you, so it is meant to be messy, loose, and fun.

Grab some paper and either markers, colored pencils, or crayons. Draw out a series of three boxes on your paper, like in a large comic.

In the first box, draw an illustration representing yourself in the past. It can be abstract, literal, a design, a symbol, or a mix of colors—whatever feels blissful. In the second box, create an image to represent you now in the present. In the third box, create an image all about you in the future. Make these really fun!

How does it feel to look at yourself through time with the eyes of your inner child? Is it thrilling, scary, fun, boring, enlivening, or relaxing? You can use this activity to explore how you can be joyful now by being present and how you can be joyful in the future by claiming your life. Find the goodness of your past and try to let the rest go as best you can. Let this miniature life review help you be light and free. Step into being a capable adult with a gorgeous sense of childlike wonder. Embrace your past, as much as you can, to craft a blissful present and future.

Release the baggage of the past. Carry joy instead.
#joyfulliving101

79. SHARING Leads to Happiness

*Affirmation: "I share my love and gratefully accept love
as it flows back to me."*

You can become a happiness junkie in a healthy way by noticing
when good feelings crop up and what elicited them. It could be
an activity, a situation, a person, a personal choice to be positive,
or something else. Those magical ingredients are your path to an
enchanting, evocative, rich, robust life of bliss.

Often happiness occurs when you are giving of yourself. If
you are connecting, sharing, and giving your love, it naturally
comes back to you, and before you know it, you are feeling deep
happiness. Getting out and being with others who care for you
and for whom you care leads to good feelings, dissipates loneliness, and causes happy moments.

Exercise: Giving and Sharing

In this exercise you will think of how you can give of yourself.
This is a powerful happiness enhancer because when you give
of yourself, you don't have time to think about how your boss
is irritating you or how you are worried about your boyfriend.

You are busy engaging with life and sharing your bounty. Giving shines a light on how abundant you really are.

There are endless ways to give and share your own inner goodness. In your journal, make a list of ways you can give back. Here are some ideas: volunteer at a local charity, share your expertise with someone just starting out in your field, send a loving greeting card to a dear friend, or put together a special homemade gift for a treasured family member. Share your joy with animals by volunteering at your local animal shelter or hugging and loving your pets or others' pets.

Choose one or two items from your list that interest you, and commit to doing one or more today. When you give and share, you tap into your love for others as well as yourself. That love naturally spills over to you.

> *Giving from the heart lights a flame of kindness,*
> *forever illuminating your world.*
> *#joyfulliving101*

80. get sensual

Affirmation: "My senses are alive with pleasure and joy."

One of the fastest ways to tap into your inner bliss is to get in touch with your senses. Your senses bring your world to life. They enliven you and make your life Technicolor. Our senses give us information all of the time, but they are an often untapped reservoir of joy and enjoyment we could have in our lives. One of the reasons we are here in human bodies is to enjoy the experience of duality and of having a body. The sights, sounds, smells, tastes, and sensations of being human are a rich, satisfying cacophony of potential pleasure and enjoyment.

Feeling good and experiencing pleasure are important ways to live a rich and satisfying life. Imagine how good you feel when you take the time to see a gorgeous art exhibit or to listen to beautiful music. These are easy ways to engage your senses and feel enlivened.

Exercise: Awaken Your Five Senses

In order to find the joy that comes from sensory pleasure in a healthy manner, we will create an exhaustive list of sense-enlivening activities. The idea is for you to do something to engage your senses every day to help you have a rich and full life. The novelty of engaging your senses will also trigger your brain to generate more feel-good chemicals, which help make you generally happier.

Grab your journal and a pen or colorful markers. You are going to make a list of at least twenty-five ways you can engage your five senses pleasurably. What will be pleasurable to see, hear, smell, touch, and taste?

Here are some ideas you can use for your list: make icy snow cones, swim in an ocean or lake and feel the water caress your skin, walk in a field and smell flowers and grass, fill your windowsills with glasses full of water with different blends of food coloring, walk barefoot in the grass or on the beach, spend time in the forest and touch the majestic rough bark of different types of trees, dance to your favorite songs with the windows open to let in the fresh air, have a lemonade- and sorbet-tasting party with friends, melt ice cubes on your lover's body, look at the passing colors of nature as you drive down a country road, and try skinny dipping on a hot night.

Look at your list and pick one thing to do now. Go back to it each day and try to do another activity. Take ownership of your enjoyment of life and make a commitment to experience life's pleasure on a daily basis. When you are enjoying life and are in touch with your body, you radiate more confidence and feel happier.

Our senses are the lavish gift of being human.
#joyfulliving101

81. change apprehension to joy

*Affirmation: "I let new experiences enliven my being
and awaken new, amazing parts of my being.
I experience life with joy and receive its bliss."*

When I was in my late teens, I visited my friend Kelly, who worked at Disney World in Florida. We went to the newest water park at the time, Typhoon Lagoon. We got to an activity in which guests wore masks and snorkels and swam over a massive tank of tropical fish.

I'd never been snorkeling before. I was nervous because the tank was full to the brim with fish. Would they move out of the way? Would they touch me and be slimy? I got in and they were so vivid and so close that I had a primal reaction. I jumped out of the water onto a rock, shrieking.

My best friend came up on the rock, took my hand, and said, "I know you are going to like this. Come in." We got back in and swam through, holding hands, and she was right. I loved it. We went though again, and I gained confidence around the fish and in the water.

Later in life, I moved to Hawaii. I snorkeled daily and learned to skin-dive deep into the sea among fish, dolphins, and even sharks. Snorkeling became, and still is, one of my top bliss-inducing activities. But if I had not tried it in Disney and had a supportive friend to walk me through it, I would never have known.

Trying something new every week or even every day enlivens your life like nothing else. Newness in any arena of life brings excitement, exhilaration, and engagement. It wakes us up and attracts our attention. Too often we are on autopilot, cruising through life only partially attentive. New experiences remind us we haven't seen it all, no matter our age. Choose to utilize this simple path to bliss and try new things!

Exercise: Commit to New Experiences

Are you willing to commit to doing something new every week? Are you interested in feeling revitalized every week? Can you imagine feeling excited by life? Does that sound good to you? Then this is the activity for you! Commit to doing something new every week. This can be anything you choose. You are empowered to choose the exciting life experiences you want to explore. Here are a few suggestions:

+ Try a new type of restaurant, maybe Ethiopian, Korean, or one hundred percent organic.
+ Find a board game you have never played and gather some friends. It could be anything from a group card

game like pinochle to a solitaire game like mahjong, or from *Dance Dance Revolution* to giant Jenga.

+ Experience a massage.

+ Create a new decoration for your home. Maybe you could create a silk flower arrangement or paint a salvaged picture frame to match your decor.

+ Meditate on a single, lively color and wear it for the day. For example, try to create a fuchsia or lemon-yellow day for yourself.

+ Watch a happy movie you have never seen.

+ Try a new sport. Never roller-skated? Get on the rink! Are you a football virgin? Try tossing the pigskin.

Life is a marathon, not a sprint. The attainable, fun challenge for you is to sustain this practice of doing something new every week. You could keep a list in your journal of your new experiences. Go over them sometimes. Some will trigger amazing moments, like that time you parasailed over an exotic beach. Some will evoke joyful memories of small moments, like trying a new flavor of snow cone with your spouse and laughing at your blue tongues. New moments add spice and variety to a joyful, beautiful life like yours.

Novelty keeps us engaged and incites our chemicals of happiness to fire and snap with bliss.
#joyfulliving101

82. Look and you'll find it

Affirmation: "*I look for beauty every day and find it everywhere. My bliss is enhanced!*"

Every day, life gifts you beauty. There is a moment, at least one and likely many, where beauty is staring you in the face. Can you find it? It's easy when you know to look. Start with the last interaction you had with another person. What moment during it was beautiful? Was it the loving greeting? Was it the hug at the end? Was it the fact that you were petting their cute dog during the conversation? Beauty is everywhere, and there is an abundance of both obvious beauty and subtle beauty to be appreciated.

What about the beauty between two people you know who have relationship issues? Is their learning and personal growth poignantly beautiful to you? How about the beauty of the productive day's work done by the gardeners in your neighborhood? Yes, they create beauty. And it feeds their souls even though it is sometimes laborious.

An attitude of optimism can help you uncover daily beauty. This enhances your bliss and makes your life more joyful and rich. You really can't go wrong with the optimistic pursuit of daily beauty. Your life will be richer and more fulfilling for it. Your reason for being will be clearer too.

Exercise: Look Closely

In this activity you are going to be writing about things of beauty at various points in your life. This will start getting you in the habit of noticing beauty in everything around you, which will nourish your spirit.

Get your journal and a writing instrument. Think back to yesterday. Choose one or more moments or experiences of beauty to list. Subtle or obvious beauty is good. Reflect on today and do the same.

Next, think back five years. Identify any day you can remember. It might be for positive or less-than-positive reasons. On that day, what beauty did you experience?

There need not be a story attached to the rest of the day. Just name the beauty. That is all. Take that with you; release your attachment to the rest.

Think back to high school. What was a moment when you experienced beauty? Write about just the beauty; the rest is in the past. The energy of the beauty can nourish you for life, though.

Last, reflect back on your childhood. Don't get caught up in judging if it was good or bad. Just let a moment of beauty come to you and make a note of it.

Throughout your life, there is beauty. It is available to nourish your spirit in perpetuity. You can let everything go, but keep the good, nourishing, joyful energy. Now that is finding bliss!

Find the beauty in situations where it is not obvious,
and you will create voluminous joy in your life.
#joyfulliving101

83. Grateful Living

Affirmation: "I live a grateful life, and the result is pure joy and happiness."

Living a grateful life can guarantee you higher levels of passion, joy, happiness, and sparkle in your life. When you live gratefully, you live in the moment. You make time for playing because you feel grateful for the good feelings it inspires. You feel more radiant because you give and share and are grateful.

Being grateful on a regular basis requires confidence in the power of gratitude. When you dare to be confident that your gratitude can change your life and the world, you attract more goodness to you. You realize that life is a treasure and so are you. You see the richness in each experience. You create paradise on earth for yourself.

Living from a place of gratitude gives you freedom to explore, feel, love, and be grateful for all the success and abundance you have received. When you're grateful, you're nurtured by what you are grateful for. So if you are grateful for nature, nature will nurture you back. If you're grateful that you are able to be yourself, you'll experience the endless possibilities that your own being can create. If you're grateful for beauty, you'll see more beauty in your life every day. If you're grateful for passionate experiences, you'll magnetize more and more possibilities for endless, sublime, sexy, passionate experiences to come to you. If you're grateful for the light and the love in your life, you will magnetize more of that in a fresh, pure, and even luxurious way. Gratitude is one of the most powerful forces for creating a blissful life. It's so sensational because it can bring forward inspiration and restoration; you recognize how wonderful your life is and affirm it by being grateful.

Even when life gives you lemons, if you choose to be grateful for them and then take the initiative to make lemonade out of them, you are embodying resourceful gratitude. And being a force of living gratitude is how to find your calling, find love, be fully present in every moment, and enjoy the ride. Gratitude directly creates happiness and bliss.

Exercise: Your Gratitude Style

Take this quiz to find out the flavor of gratitude that resonates for you.

1. How would you most like to thank your spouse, partner, or friend for supporting you through a tough week at work?

> A. By giving a heartfelt gift, like flowers with a nice note or something small and special they had their eye on

B. By making a card with a long, loving ode of your appreciation

C. By cooking their favorite meal and watching their favorite movie

2. What is your favorite way to be thanked?

    A. With a cute little gift that shows that the friend knows what you love and took the time to give it to you

    B. With e-mails and letters of appreciation that extol the gratitude in words that touch the heart

    C. By being surprised by a fun outing, like roller-skating, a great hike, or a trip to see your favorite movie

3. What does the ultimate thank-you card look like?

    A. It has a design and creativity, and it sparkles. The graphics are exciting and enchanting.

    B. The words on the front truly and lyrically express the gratitude that you feel for the exact person you're giving the card to.

    C. This card is about doing. It urges the receiver to get out and treat themselves because the giver is thankful for their help.

Answer Key

Mostly As

If you picked mostly As, your gratitude style is one of giving and receiving small, heartfelt gifts. If you have a physical token in front of you, it really drives home the point that you are being thanked, and you like to share that same kind of gratitude in a physical form with others.

Mostly Bs

If you picked mostly Bs, you are a wordsmith. You like to share your appreciation and thankfulness through words, written or spoken. You like to receive appreciation through words and have the cause and feeling of gratitude be clearly and meticulously delineated. You can use words to thank others and really communicate how grateful you are.

Mostly Cs

If you picked mostly Cs, you are a doer and a person of action. Therefore, you prefer to give and receive gratitude through action and through sharing your time and effort. You like to receive gratitude in the form of people participating in something with you or doing something for you. You like to give gratitude the same way by doing something to make someone's life easier or by sharing time together while being active.

You can use your gratitude style to live an even more grateful life. You can certainly put emphasis on your main gratitude style, but at the same time you can also focus on offering gratitude in all forms. You can be a well-rounded, grateful person sharing your thankfulness in a wide variety of ways.

There are endless ways to thank the people who have contributed to your life. Dole out thanks, and your life will bloom.
#joyfulliving101

84. hive of happiness

Affirmation: "The joy of the bee tribes infuses my life with sweetness."

According to PBS's *NOVA* website, the bee communicates through dance. This animal is a symbol of abundance, femininity, and the sweetness of life. From sacred Egyptian sites decorated with bee imagery to bees in ancient Greek myth and stories, cultures have revered the bee since antiquity. Further back in ancient times, the bee goddesses dripped honey, sharing their abundance and goodness with all.

In the book *Clan of the Goddess: Celtic Wisdom and Ritual for Women*, the author, C. C. Brondwin, explains that the Celts loved bees because they used honey to produce mead, a sweet and intoxicating drink that they enjoyed and believed helped them connect with otherworldly spirits. Mead is associated with the goddess Medb, sometimes referred to as Maebh or Maeve.

If we look at all this mythology, we find that it focuses on sweetness and goodness and on the femininity and abundance associated with bees. We can easily extrapolate how bees created a form of bliss. Something sweet and enchanting can help us feel a sense of it: the senses are pleased and engaged.

When we honor the sacred feminine and acknowledge our abundance, we feel good. Pleased. We feel full and rich in a life of diverse bounty and beautiful feminine energy, no matter what our gender might be.

Tap into the joy of the bees in the hive of happiness today! Open your heart to the sweetness of life.

Exercise: The Sweet Way

Joy is found in the sweetness of life. You can experience it right now. Enjoy this activity to tap into your own joyful sweetness.

Gather honey and a spoon. If you do not have any honey in the house, you can imagine this sweet, delicious taste. Get comfortable and lie down.

Take a little taste of honey. Place it in your mouth, hold it there for a while before you swallow it, and close your eyes. Bring your singular attention to the sweetness of the honey in your mouth. Allow the honey to gently alter your consciousness. Let yourself begin to feel the home of the hive that created this honey. The more wild and raw your honey is, the better this will work.

As you lie there with your eyes closed, envision yourself miniaturized inside a humming hive of bees. Feel yourself resting on the honeycombs. Let your sense of spirit-smell take in the ambrosial scent all around you. You can even imagine you are eating some of the honey that surrounds you, or you could even envision yourself rubbing it on your arms and legs like a soothing spa cream.

Feel yourself absorbing the essence of the hive around you. Absorb the pollen, the honeycomb, the honey, and the hum of the bees. Let yourself connect with the bees that inhabit the hive. Feel them surround you gently, lovingly.

Physically hold your hands out as you lie there with your eyes closed and feel the bees of the hive gather on your hands, their feet gently kissing your skin. These bees love you. They will only help you and never harm you. Let your hands absorb the hum and the energy of the bees. Take it into your body. Let all of these sensations crash together in a wave of joy.

Let yourself feel the happiness of the hive. Everyone is in unity here. All of the bees are a team. Stay here as long as you would like and absorb their bliss.

When you are ready, you can begin to bring your awareness back to the room and carry the sweetness you experienced with you throughout your day. Feeling the sweet essence of the honey and bees lets this effervescence be awakened within you so it can flavor your life with joy.

Embrace the sweetness of life
like a gift of honeycomb from the hive.
#joyfulliving101

85. paint your Lover

Affirmation: "*I let my love for all flow through art,
and I express how I feel.*"

Love ignites your creativity in a way that brings forward your romantic and lyrical nature. Love makes you crave beauty. It makes you desire to create harmony and melody, passion and caring. When you feel love, a cacophony of bliss chemicals engulfs you. You can harness those inner biological resources and feel blissful—that's what they're for!

Invoking the feeling of love opens the heart. In this chapter you will combine love and creativity. Doesn't that sound like ultimate bliss?

The act of painting stirs the subconscious. Using a semi-liquid medium to smear color and shape on a blank canvas allows you to express your inner emotional state and allows your subconscious and unconscious to come out to play.

This is so healthy for you! You need emotional outlets in your hectic world. Your subconscious needs a chance to be seen in the light, and your unconscious benefits greatly from your attention. Painting is healthy and bliss-inducing for you, so what about combining love and painting? Imagine the heart-centered expression that can happen!

Exercise: Paint Your Lover

Focus on the feeling of love while painting in this activity. You can do this alone or with a romantic partner.

If you are doing this activity on your own, you are your love. Self-love is the most important ingredient to a blissful life. Remember that, and use this activity to love yourself. If you are doing this activity with a romantic partner, then you will paint as you think of your love for one another. You'll really notice the love you feel for this other person opening the doors to all of the love within you.

Gather your paints, brushes, water, and canvases or paper. Use whatever you have on hand. Focus on the love you feel either for yourself or your partner. If you are doing this by yourself, look in the mirror and feel your self-love, and then go into your art area. If you're doing this with a romantic partner, gaze at your partner with love and begin to paint what you feel, not what you think.

Use the colors to express the love that you feel for yourself, your partner if you have one, and the world. Immerse yourself in the feeling of love, let go, and mix colors. You may find yourself painting with your hands instead of brushes. Go with that. Let a deep part of yourself be expressed in the activity.

Feel love and the bliss that is truly, completely flowing through you. Immerse yourself in it for this time, and enjoy the safety and bliss of deep love.

Your love is the essence of divine artistry.
Use prismatic hues to express it and shower it everywhere!
#joyfulliving101

86. sense of sensitivity

*Affirmation: "I embrace my sensitivity
and let it enhance my joy every day."*

Do you consider yourself a sensitive person? How sensitive? Are you the type of person who feels deeply every day? Are you the type of person who sometimes finds a bright, noisy environment overstimulating? Are you the type of person who feels connected to nature and beauty when things are peaceful?

If you answered yes to any of those questions, you are sensitive. And I'm betting you answered yes to at least one, because at heart we are all sensitive people. Every human is sensitive. Different factors in our lives may or may not have squeezed some of that sensitivity out of us. For better or worse, we live in a society that doesn't always prize sensitivity; it might even consider it a weakness.

The truth is that being sensitive is an enormous strength. It takes courage and inner power to be unapologetically sensitive in a world that tells you to be tough, to acquire more, to race for better status, to look better. Standing in your power, exhibiting your sensitivity, and letting sensitivity translate into kindness, caring, and emotional connection with the world around you is highly courageous. It's far more courageous than trying to hide the sensitive heart within you.

Being sensitive is a talent. You may have heard of the term a "sensitive." A sensitive is an intuitive or psychic person and is in touch with their senses more deeply than the average person. A person with this particular quality receives more elevated emotional information.

Being sensitive is actually a superpower. Embracing your sensitivity is recognizing some major talents, skills, and unique propensities within you. Sensitivity can translate into a blissful life because loving your sensitive side increases your self-love. Self-love is a critical ingredient in a blissful life.

Exercise: How Sensitive Are You?

Use this quiz to determine how sensitive you are and how to use your sensitivity and your practical side to create your ultimate bliss.

1. When you hear about a disturbing news story, does it stick with you for days or even weeks?

    A. Yes, all the time.

    B. Yes, once in a while.

    C. Not really, I'm pretty good at blocking that stuff out.

2. When you encounter a wild animal in nature, do you feel connected to it in the sense that you are confident about its state and any danger it may pose?

> A. Sometimes I can tell based on its body language and the noises it is making.
>
> B. If I see a wild animal that is potentially threatening, I always steer clear of it.
>
> C. Yes, most of the time I can usually tell if it is safe to stay near the animal or not.

3. Have you been moved to awestruck tears by a piece of music or a painting?

> A. Once or twice.
>
> B. Oh yes, certain songs really get me!
>
> C. Not really. I appreciate the arts though.

4. When a close friend or family member experiences a major life change, do you feel the emotional effects? Can you sense how they're feeling?

> A. Definitely. I share their happiness and tears.
>
> B. I definitely understand where they are mentally and am able to respond appropriately, but I don't let it affect my emotional state.
>
> C. Sometimes I can really feel what they are feeling, and sometimes I just try to be there for them in whatever way is best.

5. When you witness a moment of great beauty, do you feel soaring joy in the center of your chest?

   A. Not really.

   B. I have felt that a few times before.

   C. Yes, I know that feeling very well!

Answer Key

To score your test, add up your points.

   1. A=3, B=2, C=1
   2. A=2, B=1, C=3
   3. A=2, B=3, C=1
   4. A=3, B=1, C=2
   5. A=1, B=2, C=3

5–8: The Pragmatist

You are very practical and logical. This is a great asset because you have really good boundaries. These boundaries keep you emotionally secure and safe and help you not be overly affected by others. If you wanted to work on something, it could be continuing to cultivate compassion. Finding the balance between pragmatism and caring will bring you ultimate bliss.

9–11: The Balancer

You are able to strike a reasonable balance between your head and heart. Although you are sensitive, you also have a logical and pragmatic side. This is a good way to be because you're able to have great boundaries and yet also experience the heart-centered aspects of the world. Keep up the good work. Continue to walk the line of sensitivity and being grounded and you will keep living your joy!

12–15: The Sensitive

Being sensitive is a talent and asset. It's important for you to remember this. Most likely you were born this way. Use your sensitivity and the intuition and emotional intelligence that it gives you to better your life. Find ways to harness this talent. At the same time, make sure you have great boundaries in place. It doesn't enhance your bliss to get bummed out every time you see a sad commercial. Striking a balance between the day-to-day world and the world of feelings and emotions will bring you ultimate joy.

Being sensitive is a gift that fosters peace.
Help create a kinder, gentler world by embracing it.
#joyfulliving101

87. Loving Life Guides

Affirmation: *"My life guides offer me comfort, solace, joy, love, and bliss. I gratefully accept it, as needed, for my highest good and the highest good of all life."*

In the eternal world of nonphysical reality, there are loving, joyful, benevolent beings everywhere. And around each human being, there are many of these beings. Some of these beings or guides come into the human's sphere for a period of time; some come for a specific purpose or specific thing with which they can help the person. And some of these guides commit to being with the person for their entire life. These are called life guides.

Your life guides chose to be with you as loving supporters, cheering you on for your entire life. They are always benevolent, always positive, and always for your highest good. They're just wonderful helpers!

Because they spend your entire life with you, they really know you very well. And your health and happiness are one of their top priorities. Being a life guide is a job that these beings all love. They take it on when you incarnate, and they stay with you for your whole life. They meet you after you transition and guide you forward for your soul's next adventure.

You might wonder what they get out of this deal. They get to know you! They get to help you. They get the experience of being a life guide. It gives them a unique opportunity to have that special experience, just like you get a unique and special experience by being human.

Life in both physical and nonphysical reality is about experience and joy. It's all about love. Life guides are expert purveyors of love, and they love bliss!

Your life guides want you to feel as much bliss as possible. They want to shower you with joy. They want to encompass you with radiance. All you need to do is let them.

As you expand your perception to be aware of your life guides, you are able to take in and integrate more bliss and more joy. You're able to feel more love. You are able to accept more support and nurturance from the heart of the universe.

Exercise: Meet Your Life Guides

Sit in a comfortable place and close your eyes for a few minutes. Let your mind quiet down. Disconnect from your smartphone put it outside the room. Turn off the television. Sit in silence, and let your mind wind down. It might take a few minutes. That is okay.

Do you need something to do or think about? If you can't stop your thoughts, use a mantra. Pick one word, like "joy," "love," "bliss," or "peace." You can pick whatever word resonates for you and then repeat that word rhythmically and gently and in your mind to give your thoughts something to latch on to. Sit with your mantra or quiet thoughts for a few minutes.

Now that you are in a receptive space, with your eyes closed say aloud, "I now connect with my life guides for my highest good and the highest good of all life and in accordance with universal natural law, helping all and harming none."

Allow yourself to feel your life guides gently entering the room and stepping forward. They are lined up in front of you. Invite them to step forward and introduce themselves one at a time. Start getting used to talking to them. You can do this aloud or with your mind. If you feel silly doing this, just give it a try and you might get used to it.

When guide number one steps forward, reach out your hand as if you are going to shake hands in slow motion. Feel that happen and say hello. The life guide will say hello back. Go through and do this one, two, or three more times.

You will sense how many guides are lined up to introduce themselves today.

You may have many more life guides than the ones who stepped forward today. They do not want to overwhelm you. You can meet them all in time.

You can address your life guides and talk to them about things that are going on in your life or things that you would like help with. You can also ask them if there's anything that you can help them with. Being polite is appreciated in the spirit world, just like here, so always thank your guides. Show them love and kindness, and it will return manifold! Experience the bliss of connecting with your extended nonphysical family.

A benevolent universe of spirit helpers sits at the ready to support your unfolding joy. All you have to do is ask.
#joyfulliving101

88. TRUE safety

Affirmation: "I trust life and live deep bliss and comfort in each moment."

Imagine diving off a cliff and knowing that you would only hit gentle, comfortable clouds. Imagine softness at play with color as you fall through the air with no safety net except ultimate trust. What would that feel like?

That's what life is really like. Our souls speed through the atmosphere and land in our bodies. Then we commence a grand adventure. It has ups and downs and twists and turns like we may have never imagined. Through it all we feel, we have no safety net, yet we have the ultimate one: universal love.

Everything that happens is a dive into the abyss of love. The challenges, the fruitfulness, the joys—it's all the dance of love. Our souls took a chance by coming here. Sometimes just acknowledging this truth gives our soul and our spirit a little breathing room. It gives us a chance to relax. Within the dream of human life, finding solace, comfort, and joy are the ingredients that set the stage to experience bliss.

Feeling amazing depends on trust. Trusting yourself is absolutely paramount. Trusting life is our challenge at times, but it is also our salvation. Life wants to steer us toward bliss. Life offers us chances to grow. Life is a web of interconnected realities, offering us a chance to experience living joy in different ways, times, and places. Life is a buffet of diversity. You can partake of it and experience bliss.

Exercise: Valleys and Peaks

Have you heard of the archetype of the Fool in tarot? The Fool dances forward on the path of life, sees a cliff, and dances right off it in total trust. Throughout the fall, the Fool experiences a diverse array of experiences, but in some traditions, the Fool is safe and embraced in the light of love in the end.

Get out your journal now and write the story of the Fool for your life. You were born to your parents and stepped off the cliff into life. Write about your ups and downs, the joys, and the tough moments. End the story with how the Fool is actually the wisest, most ancient being of light you could ever imagine. And the Fool is embraced by the heart of love.

The story is true, and it's completely yours. Take the time as you write this to work through your life and stand in trust. You can experience bliss and feel amazing because you are the wisest fool who ever lived.

Every peak and valley of your life has led you to deeper understanding and, ultimately, growing compassion.
#joyfulliving101

89. COUNT YOUR BLESSINGS

Affirmation: "I am creative, blissful, and blessed!"

Every day you're blessed with hundreds of beautiful and amazing moments. Today it's your job to notice them. Really think about the gifts your life brings every day. Think of all the people you care about, the amazing experiences you've had, all the beauty and enjoyment you've experienced and seen. Flip back through your memory and rewitness some of the peak experiences in your life. Count your blessings. Having a positive view of your life will make your life more positive. Your perception is your reality, and how you choose to view your life is what makes it the way it is. You are the architect of your world and reality, and you can build it as you choose with your consciously chosen thoughts, words, and actions.

Exercise: Blessed Bliss Balloons

It is time to do a fun, silly, and fresh craft. You're going to be counting your blessings in a new way to help you view your life more positively. Balloons are seen as objects of childhood joy and fun, reminders of purity of the heart, and are our chosen shape.

Gather up some colored pieces of construction paper. Choose your very favorite colors. Cut out large, oval-shaped balloons from your papers. Take some pieces of yarn and use scotch tape to affix them at the bottom of the ovals as the strings for your balloons.

Next, decorate each balloon with one or more statements of the blessings in your life. For example, one balloon might be about your friends, and you could write "my amazing friends" on the balloon along with all their names. You could also add "new friends soon to come."

Once you have decorated all your balloons with words and phrases counting your blessings, arrange them into a bunch. It will be flat but still look like a cluster of balloons.

Use tape or staples and attach the balloons together so that you have one big bunch of two-dimensional balloons.

Put your balloons somewhere you'll see them every day, maybe in your bedroom. They will give you a chance to joyfully and beautifully count your blessings every single day.

Acknowledging your blessings makes them proliferate.
#joyfulliving101

90. you are ageless

Affirmation: "I embrace my experience and value my wisdom."

A client of mine named June appeared to be a happy, confident woman in her early sixties. She shared a story with me about how after she and some of her friends turned fifty, they felt as if they became invisible. The sometimes flattering, sometimes annoying attention paid to women by men suddenly vanished. The change was debilitating. Was she valid anymore? Valued? Had she become totally invisible? She said some of her friends chased youth with Botox and facial peels and never let a carbohydrate pass their lips. She questioned if they were happier. She told me how she considered following suit and even tried Botox. Ultimately, she decided to embrace herself and her unique beauty and not focus on youth, even though she was bombarded by images of it every day from the media.

June was marching to the beat of her own drum in more ways than one. She returned to a favorite hobby, playing the drums, and ended up joining a retirees rock band! She was living and enjoying life, and she noticed that the more she threw herself headfirst into life, the more alive she felt. Her grown kids were proud and lovingly amused. She was happy and had found her way into her next stage of life as a wise woman.

Age can ripen your body, mind, heart, and spirit to a gorgeous sheen of experienced perfection. You've learned what makes you happy. You know what warms your soul. You know more about what enlivens you. Now all you need to do is commit to it.

What are three things you can do this week to embrace who you are and joyfully own your age and experience as the valuable assets they are? They could be things like getting back to a favorite hobby, as June did. Maybe you love clothes and shopping and can help a friend find the perfect outfit for her big presentation. Perhaps you could volunteer to mentor young people in your field or coach a little league team if you were a sports star in high school.

What would be your version of June's return to the drums? How can you commit to doing one of these ideas this week? What steps will you take?

Exercise: Be a Happy Kid Regardless of Your Age

In order to embrace yourself at any age, you need to reconnect to your inner wellspring of vitality. Youth has nothing to do with true inner vitality. That comes from within, and joy multiplies it. In this exercise we will get in touch with the free and easy qualities of a child and bring them into our lives at any age. This will help us experience true liveliness and vivacity.

Children live in an unfiltered state. They let you know what they like and what they don't. Isn't that refreshing? For the most part, no one has to guess what a child thinks about something. What if you adopted the traits of a happy child? What would you say that you otherwise wouldn't? The only rule is it must be kind. Besides that, why not tell your friend you don't like peas before she cooks dinner, instead of being nice and pushing them around your plate later? Why not be honest? Focus on the fun.

You know what else kids do? They repeat what feels good and is fun. They run through the sprinkler on a hot day over and over and over because it's fun. They don't think, "Oh, I should go start the laundry" or "I really ought to go wash the car today." They go for it. They relentlessly seek fun and you should too, no matter if you are ten years old or one hundred years old. Be a fun-seeking human first and a responsible adult second. Kids choose healthy fun because that's what they know. Go that route.

> *Embrace wisdom and relentlessly pursue joy,*
> *and you can live agelessly.*
> *#joyfulliving101*

91. spiritual romance

Affirmation: "*I choose spiritual romance. I am sacred!*"

Reawaken the sacred in your love life and find the joy in romance. Spiritual romance is for you if you are looking for a new paradigm in relationships and you want to create more self-love in your life. Self-love is the key to healthy romance.

In this case spiritual doesn't mean religious. It means conscious, mindful. Maybe you like yoga and helping preserve the environment, and you are also self-aware. You probably like to explore different forms of spirituality, like Chinese medicine and Taoism, Ayurveda and Hindu culture, or Unity Churches.

To practice spiritual romance, four things must be in place. First, you must cultivate self-love. Do this by treating yourself like a treasured lover or a cherished family member, with ultimate love and kindness. Self-love is the key to a satisfying love life. Strengthen yourself to attract the best dates and relationships and have the most fun. Choose you! It is always all about you—even when it is about your love life. Everything improves when you deal self-love into the game. Your life, including your love life, grows more meaningful when you love yourself.

By loving yourself, you take the need out of relationships. Instead, you are happy and fulfilled on your own, and a great date or relationship is just the icing on the cake. With a healthy level of self-love, you guarantee your own overall happiness, dates or no dates. That same self-love transforms you into a compelling and alluring prospective partner. In the beginning of dating and relationships, an air of self-reliance and a bit of mystery make you super interesting. Your presence enhances your partner's fulfilling life and vice versa, and then you have a healthy relationship.

Second, you must consider yourself sacred. You can create a happy, healthy life by remembering that you are sacred. Sacred means precious, special, a treasure of true beauty—that's you! To do this, only make choices that honor your sacredness one hundred percent. Talk to yourself with respect and honor. Act and live the fact that you are sacred.

If you consider yourself sacred, you know you can trust yourself. You know that you are going to make great decisions that honor you. In that way, you can feel emotionally safe. You can create that for yourself. In the exercise later in the chapter, I'll help you feel how sacred you are. One of the pillars of a strong, successful life as a single person or as part of a couple is being able to have faith and trust in yourself. When you consider yourself sacred and choose actions that support that truth, you reinforce the inner belief that you truly can trust yourself. You create truth and inner strength within you. That translates into confidence and emotional safety, which then become comfort with yourself and your world.

Third, you must consider your romantic partner to be sacred. If you can't see your partner as sacred, then they aren't the right person for you. You can create a pleasant, loving relationship by remembering your partner is sacred and not settling for someone who doesn't see your sacredness. Sacredness is the key!

Finally, romantic partners must see themselves and you as sacred. Be observant and notice how your partner talks about her or himself. Does he or she engage in lots of negative self-talk? If so, your partner may not see him- or herself as sacred.

How does your partner treat you? Does she or he really listen, and is she or he fully present? Does he or she treat you with complete respect? Those are starting points to determine if she or he sees you and herself or himself as sacred. Listen to your intuition. You will be able to sense the vibe pretty easily.

If your partner does not clearly see you as sacred, move on. Spiritual romance will never be possible, but you deserve it. Choose a fun night out with friends instead or go to an art opening or yoga workshop. Cherish your sacredness and hold out for that in any potential relationships.

Exercise: "I Am Sacred" Meditation and Poster

Take a few minutes and sit or lie down in a peaceful spot. Quiet your mind and focus on your breathing. Let your consciousness unwind, and bring your attention to your brow center. Feel it begin to gently pulse.

Introduce a mantra. Repeat these words in your mind: "I am sacred." Each time your attention wanders, repeat the mantra again in your mind. Let yourself simultaneously relax and focus on the truth that you are sacred.

After a few minutes, return your focus to your brow center and notice pulsing there again. Next, ask your brain to absorb the knowledge that you are sacred. As you do this, allow yourself to feel a part of your head that will pulse extra and absorb this knowledge. Is it in the front? The back? Is it tingly or warm?

Now, ask your body to absorb the truth that you are sacred. Notice if a part of your body responds particularly to this. Does a part of you feel extra sensation? More heat or coolness?

Place your hands on the center of your chest and tell your heart how sacred it is. Feel it respond. Notice any sensations. Connect with your sacredness to deeply integrate it.

After you wrap up your mediation, get out some craft supplies and make a poster that says, "I am sacred." This will further affirm your sacredness. Decorate it beautifully. Hang it in your bedroom next to your bed, where you will see it every night and morning, or be more discreet by making a postcard and placing it on the computer or mirror. It will reprogram your cells each time you see it. You will read it without thinking. Even if you don't believe it at first, the message will penetrate your consciousness. See how your life changes for the better over time and how much happier you feel.

Spiritual romance is based on mutual respect and kindness.
#joyfulliving101

92. universal union

Affirmation: "I am joyfully one with all existence."

Union. What does it mean to you? Connection? Universality? What if part of what it means is that we are *all* united, even with those we don't know or maybe even don't like very much? How might that translate into your life? What if you are in union with your obnoxious coworker or your shifty ex? What if we are even in union with those who harm others? Are we all a reflection of each other?

What if we are all the same being? Ponder that. Consider it. Can you imagine it? Does it resonate?

You feel interconnection in various ways. It might be subtle or in your face, but you know you are not a complete island alone in existence. You are connected to something else, whether it's your computer, a friend, or a pet.

When you are open to feeling universal union, you can feel more bliss. This is because you internalize that you're not in opposition to a dualistic world; you are a part of it, and you belong here. You are meant to be here on earth amid all the chaos on the planet. Union lets you feel that on a deeper level. It helps you understand that on a vast soul level you chose to come here and have the experiences you have had. That can be hard to swallow sometimes. You are part of a dance of destiny and free will here on earth for a time, and then you will return to a much more expanded reality. You may have an idea of what follows this life, or you may not be sure. It is one of life's great mysteries, but we get a glimpse into the larger reality beyond duality when we feel union and when we have experiences of interconnection, love, and bliss.

Reach for an awareness of this unity. You've been a little bit asleep in your human body. Now you are awakening to endlessness, and it is amazingly glorious. With union, you can better know that you are a part of that radiance. You are a beautiful, radiant, infinite spirit. We are one.

Exercise: Feel Union

In this activity you will be exploring interaction with people you care about. This will allow you to be open to feeling the union between you and all life. As a result you will likely feel more happy and whole and less alone in the world.

Sit with your hands over the center of your chest. Think of someone you love dearly. Feel that love. Picture their face. Say to them aloud or internally, "I am you, and you are me. We are one."

How does that feel? Do you feel the love for them and yourself? Now picture a pet you've had or met and liked. Envision the pet's face in your mind. How do you feel toward it? Loving?

Wistful? Fond? Now, say to the pet aloud or in your mind, "I am you, and you are me. We are one."

Notice how that feels. Close your eyes and sense into your body. Where do you feel it pulse? Look around you for a living plant. Is there one in the room? If not, out the window do you see a tree? Look at it. Keep its image in your mind and say to it, "I am you, and you are me. We are one." What comes back from it? Close your eyes and sense what you feel. Colors? Sounds? Feelings? Tingling? Thank the beings with which you have just experienced connection. Outstretch your arms and say aloud, "I am in harmonious union with all existence for my highest good."

Bring your arms down. How does it feel? Let your body pulse in all directions with union. Absorb goodness and feel interconnection.

When you are ready, stand up; vigorously rub your arms, legs, and torso; and say, "I am _____ (your first name here). I enjoy my healthy unity with life for my highest good."

We are all the same being. Union is the true reality of existence.
#joyfulliving101

93. outdoor Dreaming

Affirmation: "The natural world sustains me and fills me with joy."

One of the top ways to find joy is to go outside. Outside you get enlivened by nature. Whether you're in snow-covered northern Canada and have to bundle up to go roll in the snow and make snow angels, or you're in Maui and can go out your door to snorkel amid tropical fish, every outdoor locale offers a plethora of opportunities for bliss and beauty. So let's get outside!

Being outside exposes you to fresh air. You breathe deeper outside, so you take in more oxygen and therefore physically feel better. When you go outside you can expand. Nothing is constraining you. You feel spacious. If it is daytime, you are awakened by natural light, which is known to alleviate some types of depression. If it's nighttime, you are wrapped in a mystical outdoor cocoon under the moon and stars or clouds and quiet.

Outdoors you interact with others. You may see neighbors on a walk, and animal friends, wild or domesticated, abound too. All these moments offer beauty.

Flora in the outdoors is particularly beautiful and blissful. You let your eyes feast on sumptuous flowers; tall, majestic trees; and textured, lovely plants. Vegetation offers you so much to appreciate in awe and wonder. Beautiful, blissful blooms and buds are joyfully waiting for you to notice them.

Exercise: Outdoor Odyssey

Go outside today or tonight with journal in hand. You have a mission: find ten beautiful outdoor things. Write down anything that strikes you as beautiful. Don't stop till you find them! You might have to keep walking or biking or driving. Seek out beauty. After you go home, write one word next to each thing on your list about how seeing, hearing, smelling, tasting, or touching it made you feel. Some examples are "awestruck," "happy," "calm," and "lucky."

Beauty evokes bliss and appreciation, and the outdoors provides bliss all the time. Get outside daily and treat yourself to beauty.

Go outside, wherever you are, and appreciate each drop of water,
each flower, each architectural work of art.
#joyfulliving101

94. GIVING IS LIVING

Affirmation: "*I let giving fill me with joy.*"

When our lives are full and abundant and we are grateful, a natural extension of that gratitude is giving. We give because we have so much. Giving brings us joy and bliss. We do it because we are internally, emotionally abundant. And sharing just feels good! Bliss and joy result because giving from the heart feels good. Try it today!

You can choose to give as a daily part of life. You can choose to share because you are grateful. You can be in the flow, feel complete, and give of yourself in an easy, gentle way and feel brighter and happier. You can choose joy through giving in gratitude.

Giving is a beautiful thing. It drives your life forward, as you are an example of living grace. It brings your life color and vividness. It incites feelings of bliss and endless caring. When you believe in a benevolent, abundant world, why would you do anything but give and shine in joy?

Have you ever heard the phrase "live to give"? If you feel that your reason for living is small or meaningless, you can live for greatness by living to give. It's the ultimate in positivity, abundance, and gratitude. It's a fresh innovation in a world of lack and fear. You can bust the system that tells you that you'll never have enough and must acquire more stuff. You can do this by affirming your endless abundance and giving and sharing in a celebration of gratitude. By doing this, you enter a new era! You step into the power of the moment where you're present, abundant, and grateful for the endless bounty in your life. Your heart can relax and open in this way. You can have confidence in the goodness of the world in which you live. And you can discover bliss each day by giving of yourself.

Giving makes you glow. It answers the call of the heart. You can donate your money or your time to a local soup kitchen or animal shelter. You can give some of your excess possessions to a local fundraising sale. But giving isn't always about money or things. Sometimes giving is offering a contact to a colleague who could use a hand up. Giving can be listening when a family member has had a rough day. And sometimes giving is picking wildflowers for someone you care about.

Exercise: How Can You Give?

Set up a page in your journal on which you list each day how you gave a gift to life. This might include things like calling a friend with kind words, doing a favor for an elderly neighbor, inviting a new friend on an activity they might enjoy, lovingly assisting someone with a task they find difficult, bringing a special treat to someone who could use a pick-me-up, mailing a "just because" card to a special friend.

Write how it felt to give each of the things you listed. Did you feel blissful, happy, or more abundant through giving? Find ways to give every day, and enhance your bliss by affirming the abundance of goodness in your life with the gratitude displayed through giving.

Every kind word or action has an equal reaction.
What you put out comes back to you.
Why not make it caring and joyful?
#joyfulliving101

95. you only live once: dare to live to the fullest

Affirmation: "I am bold and daring. I go after what I want and create massive joy in my life."

This moment, this time in your life, is rare. It will only happen one time. You've heard the saying "you only live once," haven't you? Even if technically that's not true if you favor the idea of reincarnation, the sentiment remains. You will only be who you are right now for a brief time. The real message behind the saying is go for it! Dare! Seize the day!

Whatever the day is like, it's beautiful. Look outside. It might be night, or it might be day. It might be sunny, or it might be raining. It might be dreary, or it might be vibrant. Whatever it is, it's unique and beautiful just like you. You can insert yourself into the bliss of each day. Just as you did in the "Colors of the Body" exercise in chapter 60, you can play with the colors of your world with joy and gratitude. You can invite yourself to create a world filled with vital life force and glowing, breathing, living love. You can create bliss by going for it.

What reason do you have to wait? Why would you delay sparkling? You are radiant. You sparkle. Specific experiences, activities, feelings, and situations inspire your shimmering countenance. What is the point of delaying that? Why would you wait to share your unique, mesmerizing flame of beauty? Twirl into your colors! Be bold! Acknowledge your limitlessness. Open your heart, in this moment, this day, to the singular miracle of your existence. You only live once in this body—*dare!*

Exercise: Daring Day

Today, you are going to have the most daring day you've had in a long while. I want you to list something that you are absolutely petrified to do but that you know would bring you bliss and be a positive force in your life. It could be anything from applying for a job in a completely new field to taking a bungee jumping lesson, or from going back to school to singing onstage in front of a large group. These might seem like crazy, spur-of-the-moment things to do, but chances are they're things you've been thinking about doing for a while. What do you find absolutely and simultaneously exhilarating and petrifying? Dig deep down and be honest with yourself. Think big. Honor yourself with huge thinking. Ignite your imagination and open your mind to much greater levels of vibrant bliss.

You know what's coming next, don't you? You need to do this thing. You need to commit to it and ignite the passion, boldness, and shining bright radiance within you. List the steps to make it happen. Start now. Pick up the phone. Work on your résumé. Make the appointment. Whatever it is, it's time. Dare!

Be brave and create the life of your dreams.
Dare to strive for the spectacular.
#joyfulliving101

96. the wonder of writing

Affirmation: "*I am a storyteller and experience the bliss of writing.*"

Writing is a unique and powerful form of inspiration because it takes your creative impulses and gives them words. For most of your life, you have a relatively constant narrative made of words running in your head. You think in words more often than not. You communicate in words most of the time. And so creating by writing words integrates creativity into a daily activity. Words are powerful symbols that mean many things and can be used to create absolutely anything!

Writing can be so enjoyable. Have you ever tried to create an entirely new world by writing something? Have you written fiction? It can also be wonderfully fun to write about a subject you know a lot about. Maybe writing about that beloved subject gives you joy. Or maybe you like to write a blog that reviews the latest episodes of your favorite reality show. Finding the fun and enjoyment in writing brings bliss to your daily language.

Journaling and writing about your life, your day, and your feelings is positive and powerful. It helps you express and integrate what you're feeling within. It helps you express what is inside of you using the powerful language of words.

All of these types of writing open doorways to bliss and beauty. You can jump into words and all the beauty they can express at any moment. Notice the bliss and beauty of words today.

Exercise: Creating Blissful Stories

It is time for you to explore the joy of writing. Find your bliss using this activity.

With either pen and paper or a device of some sort, craft a story. Create a protagonist (hero) and antagonist (villain) in your story. Make your story about something that excites you. It might be something that you've never tried or something that you absolutely love. Either way, write this story and be as wild and outlandish as possible. Give your story a beginning, middle, and an end. In the beginning, explain the characters. In the middle of it, share the problem that the protagonist must overcome. And at the end, the characters must surmount any obstacles and triumph. Have fun with it! Enjoy doing this completely fun, completely creative activity.

Enjoy reading your story and share it if you'd like!

Make sure to give yourself daily opportunities to express your creativity.

Tell the story of your life with grace and candor.
Sharing your wisdom helps others and delivers deep satisfaction.
#joyfulliving101

97. emotional safety and security

Affirmation: "*I am emotionally fluid and safe.*"

Emotional safety and security are ingredients that can greatly enhance your bliss. When you feel emotionally safe and secure, you have a solid internal, emotional foundation. You truly love yourself and know that you can trust yourself. You know that you will care for yourself in a way that is for your highest good.

Being able to trust yourself to make great decisions and even to talk about yourself kindly and with self-love are amazing assets. This self-trust is the cornerstone of feeling emotionally safe. It starts within you. It's your foundation. And if you did not start your life feeling emotionally safe and secure, you can cultivate the feeling now. The first step is to love and honor yourself.

Internal, emotional safety comes from accepting the fact that you are sacred. If you believe and integrate this truth about yourself, it will change the way you think, speak, and act. It will drastically change your life for the better and help create more and more bliss.

Learn to live in a way that honors your sacredness. Only make decisions that affirm how sacred you are. Only say things about yourself that affirm your love for yourself. Watch your thoughts! Think positive, loving things about yourself and make a commitment to be conscious about treating yourself with love and sacredness. You are sacred.

Exercise: Your Positive Foundation

This activity is intended to get you to look at the positive qualities of people you admire and then at your own positive qualities. This will help you realize that you are also worthy of admiration. You can answer these questions in your journal:

- What positive core values did your immediate family pass on to you?
- Of everyone you have ever known, whom do you admire most? What makes this person worthy of your admiration?
- Name the four pillars that are your character. These are the parts of your personality and value system that you deem most important and central to who you are.
- What do you consider the most important parts of your own personal foundation (that which holds you up and makes you strong)?
- Affirm all the positive qualities you mentioned above. Write affirmations to strengthen your foundation. Say them aloud after writing them and whenever so moved. Here are some examples:
    - I am levelheaded.

- I have a large support system.
- I am a loyal friend.
- I am a positive thinker.
- I am inventive and innovative.

Say the following affirmation aloud three times: "My inner and outer foundations are strong, stable, and supportive. I empower my sacred foundation for all time. The core of my being is my strength and steadiness."

There is an exemplary pillar of inner strength within you.
Acknowledge it to embolden it to grow.
#joyfulliving101

98. nature speaks

Affirmation: *"I am nurtured into blissful radiance by nature,*
Natura, and my elemental friends."

In the sometimes confusing, sometimes exhilarating, sometimes blissful, sometimes challenging world that you live in, you have an amazing source of comfort and support right outside your door. That support comes directly from nature. Nature is right there in every tree, blade of grass, stone, pigeon, park, forest, and beach.

Nature is pulsing with life in every moment. It is part of the interconnected web of everything. For people, nature has a unique ability to foster feelings of interconnection. As you witness beauty in nature, whether it's a single feather or a huge willow tree, you feel connected to other parts of life.

Nature also brings you the experience of being outdoors—the refreshing experience of being outside and breathing fresh air. The lyrical experience of hearing wind blow through the leaves of a tree or listening to songbirds chirp an exuberant tune raises your spirit. Being outside activates your senses. Your senses can take in the bliss of the salty smell of the beach, the warmth of the sun on your skin, and the refreshing water on your toes.

The exciting thing about nature is the aliveness you get to connect to. Being outside reminds you that you are part of nature. You are connected to everything, and though you may dwell in human-built homes, once upon a time your ancestors were wild, running through forests with their hearts beating fast and hearing the call of the wild.

When you feel the wildness of your own spirit, you can connect with the fairies and elementals. These beings have every flavor of personality that you could imagine, from the wild, free, and drumbeat-loving fire elementals to the gentle and ethereal spirits of the wind, dancing with freedom.

Go outside and feel the spirits of nature today. Unfocus your eyes and let yourself take in tiny sparkles all around you. They are nature sparkles, and they're alive!

Exercise: Nurtured by Natura

Natura is a goddess. She was revered during the Middle Ages and by the ancient Greeks. She was considered a representation and personification of Mother Nature. The Latin word *natura*, which means "birth," is the root word of our commonly used "nature." She was also studied by the mystic and philosopher Rudolph Steiner.

Think of Natura as the feminine spirit of nature. Earlier we met Gaia; she is the being whose body is the Earth and is a separate goddess in Greek mythology. Connecting to Natura, the feminine spirit of nature, can be a comforting and enhancing experience. Give it a try and notice how your overall connection to nature deepens.

Go outside and find a spot to sit that's comfortable and beautiful. If you have a favorite spot in nature, go there. Relax for a few minutes and quiet your mind. Meditate and feel present, simply being, while taking in the sights, sounds, smells, and feelings of nature.

Say aloud, "I invite the spirits of nature around me to display themselves to me. I come to you in love, and I ask for only the highest good."

Relax, unfocus your eyes, and open your senses. Feel the spirits of nature around you dancing and playing. Let yourself see them, hear them, smell them, feel them, sense them. Let yourself become aware of the teeming life force surrounding you. It is seen and unseen, physical and nonphysical.

Say hello to the spirits of nature. Sing, dance, and play with them. Thank them.

Then, go back to your spot and sit in the quiet communion with nature and the spirits around you. Feel recognized and validated as you rest and feel the nurturance and support of nature. Give recognition and validation back to the spirits too. They really appreciate it in a world that has partially forgotten them.

Open your heart even more and say aloud, "I now connect with Natura, the feminine spirit of all nature. I welcome the presence of this loving, benevolent, radiant goddess with an open heart for the highest good of all life." Begin to feel Natura all around you and sitting before you. Let yourself sense her presence. This is Mother Nature.

Physically open your arms in a big hug to Natura and invite her to hug you. Feel her gently move forward and enfold you in her arms. Experience this loving communion with Natura. Hug each other for as long as you'd like, and accept her nurturing energy with an open, grateful heart.

Tell her anything that you would like, and listen with all of your senses for her messages. Enjoy communing with Natura and the elementals for as long as you'd like. When you're ready, simply thank them all and state, "I now disconnect from the elementals and Natura, as needed for my highest good in love and light."

Then go about your day and maybe enjoy a fun nature walk to enhance your bliss even further.

Mother Nature offers her nurturing essence to us all freely
with no expectation of reciprocation.
#joyfulliving101

99. YOUR amazing Life

Affirmation: "I dance through life, living my bliss, steeped in joy."

You are the creator of your life. Choose the good stuff. Bliss. Abundance. Love. Fun. Harmony. Joy. Sharing. Kindness. Beauty. Radiance. Color. Grace. Aliveness. You are in control. And yet you are but a spirit, floating like a feather on gentle breezes through dimensions and realities and experiencing diverse wonder with each gust.

You can take the reins and feel amazing in any moment. You are your own guru. You are your own hero. You are the creator, the author, the writer, and even the editor of your own story. Choose one that makes you feel amazing every day.

You get to choose how to be nurtured by life. You get to relax into seductive elegance. You get to dance with freedom and joy and create your own personal paradise. You get to live in light and splash in abundant options. You get to embody the spirit and essence of your own unique bliss.

Exercise: See What Is Amazing

Sometimes it takes commitment to see your awesomeness every single day.

Turn on some music. Make it upbeat, make it uplifting, make it joyful. Turn it up loud.

Dance right now. Dance with passion and vigor. Dance away your density. Dance and dazzle yourself with the delight in the center of your soul. Dare to come alive with this dance right now.

Think about the amazing experiences you have had in your life so far. They might be the obvious kind, like having a close encounter with a beautiful deer in your backyard, or you may just think of a moment when you held hands with your child while crossing the street and she said something quirky. These types of experiences remind us of the joy of being alive. They remind us of the gift of living. Because the truth is that you live an extraordinary life. Even if it appears ordinary on the outside, if you look closer, joy and diverse experiences are all around you.

Notice how extraordinary your life truly is.
It's filled with love. Open your heart to it.
#joyfulliving101

100. HOW TO FIND JOY

Affirmation: "Joy is all around me, and I celebrate it all."

Allegria, joie, júbilo—so many ways to say joy! Joy is bursting all over the world, all the time. In every country there is joy. It may be small, personal joys of family or huge, joyful festivals of community. We live in a primarily benevolent world filled with billions of people trying to find happiness. Bliss is something universal that everyone wants. And it is everywhere. Start looking for it.

Exercise: Bliss and Joy Surround You

In order to notice that joy is all around us and all around the world, we will observe and record it. Keep a little joy notebook for three days. Take it with you and make a point each day to notice people and accomplish the mission of seeing or hearing people experiencing joy. Record these incidences in your notebook by describing them or drawing them. By actively seeking it out, you'll begin to see joy all around you!

Search your local area for opportunities for joy through community. You can do an Internet search for your state and the word "celebrations" or "festivals." Sometimes if you include the words "children," "music," or "art" in your search, you will find some great day trips. Below you will see a list of joyful gatherings. Maybe you live near one of them. If not, let this list hearten you, because happiness is happening all over the planet. Find some near you.

Here are some examples of joyful gatherings and ways people celebrate the idea of joy all over the world:

+ Agitagueda Art Festival, in which hundreds of colorful umbrellas hang over the streets, in Portugal

+ Albuquerque International Balloon Fiesta, a celebration of color and hot-air balloons

+ Electric Forest Music Festival, with its colorfully lit-up trees, in Rothbury, Michigan

+ Holi Festival, celebrating colors and joy, in India in March

+ La Tomatina, an August festival of exuberant tomato throwing, in Buñol, Spain

+ Lantern festivals, usually in February or March, in Asia

+ Mango Madness Festival and Night of 1,000 Mangos on the island of St. Lucia

+ Misty Bliss Festival in Jamaica

+ O+ Festival, which celebrates art, music, and wellness, in Kingston, New York,

+ Sizdahbedar, a day joyfully spent outdoors with family, in Iran

- Fairy and Human Relations Congress in Twisp, Washington
- Maryland Faerie Festival
- White Nights Festival, a winter festival of the midnight sun, in Saint Petersburg, Russia
- Wild Amelia Nature Festival on Amelia Island, Florida
- World Science Festival, with learning and science for all ages, in New York City

Celebrate joy and bliss today, and know that you are not alone. All around the world, people want to be joyful, feel love, and care for each other and our planet. Embrace all cultures, all flavors, all the beauty, and all the bliss this world has to offer. Share your joy.

All around the world, people are exuberantly laughing right now. #joyfulliving101

101. Joyful Living, Right Now!

Affirmation: "I am blissed out! I make time for joy every day.
I commit to seeking healthy pleasure and reveling in it."

Sometimes in our culture, pleasure-seeking and joyfulness are associated with being under the influence of alcohol or drugs. Of course, alcohol is actually a depressant, and illegal drugs are obviously unhealthy for you. So how do you find pleasure and joy? How do you get blissed-out in a good way?

You've heard the term "high on life." What if you become one of those people who feel that? What if you work at feeling good? Think about the benefits you'd reap. Instead of feeling like you are stuck in an endless daily grind, you could add some pleasure to your day *every day*.

And that means some healthy pleasure. What does that rule out for you? And more importantly, what are some of the endless possibilities for healthy pleasure you can think of?

Physical activity really amps up our pleasure principle because it releases two of the main feel good chemicals in our body: serotonin and endorphins. And it doesn't have to necessarily be vigorous or traditional physical activity. It can be splashing in puddles, taking a gentle walk, or practicing tai chi.

At the complete other end of the spectrum, you might try a high-octane dance party, bungee jumping, or a five-mile swim in the ocean. Anything physical is going to wake up your senses and optimize your body chemistry toward pleasure.

Beauty also gives us pleasure. Seeing colors and shapes put together in a pleasing arrangement, creating music, feeling the serene effect of seeing a ballet, or viewing a thrilling piece of art—these things stimulate and enliven us. And experiencing beauty releases dopamine, feel-good chemical extraordinaire.

Feelings of belonging are pleasurable too. Whether we're cheering for a favorite sports team with other fans or engaging in girl talk with a close group, when we feel like part of the pack, we feel accepted and like we belong. Feeling like we belong, overall confidence, and self-esteem are linked with serotonin, which is one of the key chemicals in our internal happiness cocktail. Serotonin helps us feel like we belong, which in turn makes us happier. A sense of belonging is a basic human need.

Exercise: How to Get Blissed Out

Blissed-out living is living life with the intention of feeling joy and spreading it to others. Some examples are laughing, dancing, and being a free spirit for the day. When you do whatever is "outside the box" for you, then you venture out of your comfort zone. That might be singing karaoke, taking salsa lessons, eating five-alarm peppers, or swimming naked. When you have outrageous fun, you are flooding your body with all kinds of natural happiness chemicals like endorphins, serotonin, and even adrenaline. Those chemicals connect the dots between our mind's experience of joy, our emotional experience of joy, and our body's physical reaction to joy. All of this combined is joyful living!

List and date ten joyful-living action steps that you could do in the next week. Write these in your journal and actually do them—all of them! Record how these actions felt and how you felt after doing them. Write about how your life changed as a result of these ten things you enjoyed.

> *You have the power to choose joyful living*
> *through your thoughts, actions, and choices.*
> *#joyfulliving101*

CONCLUSION

We have explored joy in this book from every angle! We have dipped our toes into bliss and dove headfirst into an endless sea of happiness. Joy is our natural state and how we are meant to feel. It can be challenging to open our hearts and connect our emotions for ultimate bliss in this life, but with awareness and dedication it can certainly be accomplished and even become a habit.

Our senses and our emotions are what make us uniquely human. These are the reasons that as souls we might choose to incarnate here, to have amazing experiences, and to share a blissful world with each other. I hope you find your bliss every day you work with this book. It was written as a love note to you in the hopes that you will remember what an extraordinary person you are in each moment.

This book is dedicated to you feeling good and creating a life of happiness. May joy prevail on earth—above, below, and all around for all time.

The Joy Manifesto

This manifesto is the perfect ending to a book about cultivating joy. A manifesto is an announcement of purpose, and in this case, you are announcing your commitment to cultivating bliss. As you finish up this book, or if you just opened up to this page today, it is time to proclaim your desire to be joyful. Read over the manifesto below, and if it resonates with your heart and soul, say it aloud or in your mind. Use this seemingly innocuous but powerful practice to infuse your life with bliss:

"I am a being of light. My birthright is joy. I choose impassioned living and vitality today and every day. I embody bliss and radiate it through my world. I inspire kindness, and I choose joy. I make my world a better place. Joy above me, joy below me. Joy to my left, joy to my right. Joy before me, and joy behind me. I am living bliss. I am a fountain of joy. My soul is washed clean with joy, and I am endlessly full with the bliss of the universe. It is done."

Joyful Living Toolkit

To download your free joyful living toolkit and put what you've learned in this book into action right now, go to www .amyleighmercree.com/joyfullvingtoolkit (password: JOYFUL).

acknowledgments

It takes a virtual village of talented people to turn an idea into a gorgeous book to be shared with many. I am grateful for my amazing agent, Lisa Hagan, who has been my cheerleader and a wonderful friend for many delightful years. The team of caring professionals at Llewellyn Worldwide are extraordinary. Thank you to Angela Wix for seeing the potential in my work and helping polish it and to bring it to life! Gratitude to Lauryn Heineman for her spectacular editing skills. Thank you to Vanessa Wright for helping share the joyful message of this book far and wide. And thank you to Donna Burch-Brown and Ellen Lawson for their fabulous design work.

I would also like to thank everyone who has come through my virtual office doors for medical intuitive and meet-your-spirit-guide appointments for the last fifteen years. You have all shared a facet of the glorious tapestry of life with me, and it is because of you that I can offer the joyful message that this book holds. I am grateful to have the privilege of witnessing the endless variations and poignancy of human existence.

Last but not least, I would like to thank my family, my extended family, my friends—who are family of the heart—and my husband for their love, their support, and the joy they bring to my life each day.

chapters by category

BibLioGraphy

Bergland, Christopher. "The Neurochemicals of Happiness." *The Athlete's Way* (blog). *Psychology Today.* November 29, 2012. https://www.psychologytoday.com/blog/the -athletes-way/201211/the-neurochemicals-happiness.

Brondwin, C. C. *Clan of the Goddess: Celtic Wisdom and Ritual for Women.* Wayne, NJ: Career Press, 2002.

Economou, George D. *The Goddess Natura in Medieval Literature.* Notre Dame: University of Notre Dame Press, 2002.

Nadel, Laurie. "Distant Prayer, Reiki, and Imagery Heal Ovarian Tumor." *The Inner Spiral.* Accessed December 13, 2012. http://theinnerspiral.com/distant-prayer-reiki-and -imagery-heal-ovarian-tumor/ (site discontinued).

NOVA. "Communication." *NOVA.* Accessed September 15, 2015. http://www.pbs.org/wgbh/nova/bees/hivecomm .html.

Steiner, Rudolf. *The Goddess: From Natura to the Divine Sophia.* Pocket library of spiritual wisdom. London: Rudolf Steiner Press, 2002.

Recommended Reading

Alisa Vitti, *WomanCode: Perfect Your Cycle, Amplify Your Fertility, Supercharge Your Sex Drive, and Become a Power Source*

Antero Alli, *Angel Tech: A Modern Shaman's Guide to Reality Selection*

Chad Mercree, *The Way of the Psychic Heart: Developing Your Spiritual Gifts in the Everyday World*

Christine Arylo, *Madly in Love with ME: The Daring Adventure of Becoming Your Own Best Friend*

Gabrielle Bernstein, *May Cause Miracles: A 40-Day Guidebook of Subtle Shifts for Radical Change and Unlimited Happiness*

Gary Vaynerchuk, *The Thank You Economy*

Kristine Carlson, *Don't Sweat the Small Stuff for Moms: Simple Ways to Stress Less and Enjoy Your Family More*

Linda Joy and Bryna René, *Inspiration for a Woman's Soul: Choosing Happiness*

Michael Singer, *The Untethered Soul: The Journey Beyond Yourself*

Michelle Gielan, *Broadcasting Happiness: The Science of Igniting and Sustaining Positive Change*

Shannon Kaiser, *Find Your Happy: 365 Days of Motivation for a Happy, Peaceful and Fulfilling Life* and *Adventures for Your Soul: 21 Ways to Transform Your Habits and Reach Your Full Potential*

Shirley MacLaine, *The Camino: A Journey of the Spirit*

Sue Frederick, *Dancing at Your Desk: A Metaphysical Guide to Job Happiness*

To Write to the Author

If you wish to contact the author or would like more information about this book, please write to the author in care of Llewellyn Worldwide Ltd. and we will forward your request. Both the author and publisher appreciate hearing from you and learning of your enjoyment of this book and how it has helped you. Llewellyn Worldwide Ltd. cannot guarantee that every letter written to the author can be answered, but all will be forwarded. Please write to:

Amy Leigh Mercree
℅ Llewellyn Worldwide
2143 Wooddale Drive
Woodbury, MN 55125-2989

Please enclose a self-addressed stamped envelope for reply, or $1.00 to cover costs. If outside the U.S.A., enclose an international postal reply coupon.

Many of Llewellyn's authors have websites with additional information and resources. For more information, please visit our website at http://www.llewellyn.com.